50 Pizza Variety Recipes for Home

By: Kelly Johnson

Table of Contents

- Margherita Pizza
- Pepperoni Pizza
- Hawaiian Pizza
- BBQ Chicken Pizza
- Vegetarian Pizza
- Meat Lover's Pizza
- Buffalo Chicken Pizza
- Four Cheese Pizza
- Mediterranean Pizza
- White Pizza
- Pesto Chicken Pizza
- Spinach and Feta Pizza
- Sausage and Mushroom Pizza
- Philly Cheesesteak Pizza
- Taco Pizza
- Bacon and Egg Breakfast Pizza
- Fig and Prosciutto Pizza
- Shrimp Scampi Pizza
- Artichoke and Olive Pizza
- BBQ Pulled Pork Pizza
- Chicken Alfredo Pizza
- Greek Pizza
- Caprese Pizza
- Italian Sausage and Peppers Pizza
- Roasted Vegetable Pizza
- Taco Supreme Pizza
- Bacon Cheeseburger Pizza
- Buffalo Cauliflower Pizza
- Chicken Tikka Masala Pizza
- Macaroni and Cheese Pizza
- Ratatouille Pizza
- Breakfast Burrito Pizza
- Caramelized Onion and Gorgonzola Pizza
- Mushroom and Truffle Oil Pizza
- Thai Chicken Pizza

- Smoked Salmon and Dill Pizza
- Peking Duck Pizza
- Reuben Pizza
- Chicken Shawarma Pizza
- Spaghetti and Meatball Pizza
- Tandoori Paneer Pizza
- BLT Pizza
- Eggplant Parmesan Pizza
- Pulled BBQ Jackfruit Pizza
- Crab Rangoon Pizza
- French Onion Soup Pizza
- Jerk Chicken Pizza
- Philly Cheesesteak Stuffed Crust Pizza
- Roast Beef and Horseradish Pizza
- Clam and Garlic Pizza

Margherita Pizza

Ingredients:

- 1 pre-made pizza dough (or you can make your own)
- 1/2 cup of tomato sauce (preferably made with San Marzano tomatoes)
- 8 oz fresh mozzarella cheese, sliced
- Fresh basil leaves
- Salt, to taste
- Extra-virgin olive oil

Instructions:

1. Preheat your oven to the highest temperature it can go, typically around 500°F (260°C). If you have a pizza stone, place it in the oven while it preheats.
2. Roll out your pizza dough on a lightly floured surface to your desired thickness. If you prefer a thinner crust, roll it out thinner.
3. Transfer the rolled-out dough to a pizza peel or a lightly floured baking sheet.
4. Spread the tomato sauce evenly over the dough, leaving a small border around the edges for the crust.
5. Arrange the sliced fresh mozzarella evenly over the sauce.
6. Tear the fresh basil leaves and scatter them over the cheese.
7. Sprinkle a pinch of salt over the pizza.
8. Drizzle a bit of extra-virgin olive oil over the top.
9. If you're using a pizza stone, carefully transfer the pizza from the peel to the hot stone in the oven. If using a baking sheet, simply place the baking sheet in the oven.
10. Bake the pizza for about 10-12 minutes, or until the crust is golden brown and the cheese is bubbly and slightly browned.
11. Once done, remove the pizza from the oven and let it cool for a minute or two before slicing.
12. Serve your delicious Margherita pizza hot and enjoy!

Feel free to adjust the ingredients and quantities to suit your taste preferences. Enjoy your homemade Margherita pizza!

Pepperoni Pizza

Ingredients:

- 1 pre-made pizza dough (or homemade)
- 1/2 cup of pizza sauce
- 1 1/2 cups shredded mozzarella cheese
- 20-25 slices of pepperoni
- 1/4 cup sliced black olives (optional)
- 1/4 cup sliced green bell peppers (optional)
- 1/4 cup sliced mushrooms (optional)
- 1/4 cup sliced onions (optional)
- 1/4 teaspoon dried oregano
- 1/4 teaspoon dried basil
- Red pepper flakes (optional)
- Olive oil, for brushing crust

Instructions:

1. Preheat your oven to the highest temperature it can go, typically around 500°F (260°C). If you have a pizza stone, place it in the oven while it preheats.
2. Roll out your pizza dough on a lightly floured surface to your desired thickness. Transfer the rolled-out dough to a pizza peel or a lightly floured baking sheet.
3. Spread the pizza sauce evenly over the dough, leaving a small border around the edges for the crust.
4. Sprinkle the shredded mozzarella cheese evenly over the sauce.
5. Arrange the pepperoni slices over the cheese. Add any optional toppings like olives, bell peppers, mushrooms, or onions if desired.
6. Sprinkle the dried oregano and basil over the top of the pizza. If you like it spicy, add some red pepper flakes.
7. Brush the edges of the crust with olive oil for a golden finish.
8. If you're using a pizza stone, carefully transfer the pizza from the peel to the hot stone in the oven. If using a baking sheet, simply place the baking sheet in the oven.
9. Bake the pizza for about 10-12 minutes, or until the crust is golden brown and the cheese is bubbly and slightly browned.
10. Once done, remove the pizza from the oven and let it cool for a minute or two before slicing.

11. Serve your delicious pepperoni pizza hot and enjoy!

Feel free to customize the toppings to your liking, and don't forget to adjust the baking time depending on your oven and desired crust crispiness. Enjoy your homemade pepperoni pizza!

Hawaiian Pizza

Ingredients:

- 1 pre-made pizza dough (or homemade)
- 1/2 cup of pizza sauce
- 1 1/2 cups shredded mozzarella cheese
- 8 oz. sliced ham, diced
- 1 cup pineapple chunks (fresh or canned)
- 1/4 cup sliced red onion (optional)
- 1/4 cup sliced jalapeños (optional, for a spicy kick)
- Olive oil, for brushing crust

Instructions:

1. Preheat your oven to the highest temperature it can go, typically around 500°F (260°C). If you have a pizza stone, place it in the oven while it preheats.
2. Roll out your pizza dough on a lightly floured surface to your desired thickness. Transfer the rolled-out dough to a pizza peel or a lightly floured baking sheet.
3. Spread the pizza sauce evenly over the dough, leaving a small border around the edges for the crust.
4. Sprinkle the shredded mozzarella cheese evenly over the sauce.
5. Arrange the diced ham evenly over the cheese.
6. Distribute the pineapple chunks over the pizza. If using canned pineapple, make sure to drain them well to remove excess liquid.
7. Add sliced red onions and jalapeños if desired.
8. Brush the edges of the crust with olive oil for a golden finish.
9. If you're using a pizza stone, carefully transfer the pizza from the peel to the hot stone in the oven. If using a baking sheet, simply place the baking sheet in the oven.
10. Bake the pizza for about 10-12 minutes, or until the crust is golden brown and the cheese is bubbly and slightly browned.
11. Once done, remove the pizza from the oven and let it cool for a minute or two before slicing.
12. Serve your delicious Hawaiian pizza hot and enjoy!

Feel free to customize the toppings to your liking. Some people also like to add cooked bacon or barbecue sauce for extra flavor. Enjoy your homemade Hawaiian pizza!

BBQ Chicken Pizza

Ingredients:

- 1 pizza dough (store-bought or homemade)
- 1/2 cup barbecue sauce (use your favorite kind)
- 1 cup cooked chicken, shredded or diced
- 1 cup shredded mozzarella cheese
- 1/4 cup red onion, thinly sliced
- Fresh cilantro leaves, chopped (optional)
- Olive oil (for brushing)

Instructions:

1. Preheat your oven to the temperature specified on the pizza dough package or recipe (usually around 425°F or 220°C).
2. Roll out the pizza dough on a lightly floured surface to your desired thickness. Transfer the dough to a lightly greased baking sheet or pizza stone.
3. Brush the surface of the dough lightly with olive oil. This will help create a golden crust and prevent the toppings from making the crust soggy.
4. Spread the barbecue sauce evenly over the dough, leaving a small border around the edges for the crust.
5. Sprinkle the cooked chicken evenly over the barbecue sauce.
6. Scatter the shredded mozzarella cheese over the chicken.
7. Arrange the sliced red onions on top of the cheese.
8. If desired, sprinkle chopped cilantro leaves over the pizza for extra flavor.
9. Bake the pizza in the preheated oven for about 12-15 minutes, or until the crust is golden brown and the cheese is bubbly and melted.
10. Once done, remove the pizza from the oven and let it cool for a few minutes before slicing.
11. Slice the pizza, serve, and enjoy!

Feel free to customize the toppings to your preference. You can add cooked bacon, sliced bell peppers, jalapeños, or any other ingredients you like on your pizza.

Vegetarian Pizza

Ingredients:

- 1 pizza dough (store-bought or homemade)
- 1/2 cup pizza sauce or marinara sauce
- 1 cup shredded mozzarella cheese
- 1/2 cup sliced bell peppers (red, green, and/or yellow)
- 1/2 cup sliced mushrooms
- 1/4 cup sliced black olives
- 1/4 cup sliced red onions
- 1/4 cup sliced cherry tomatoes
- 1/4 cup sliced fresh basil leaves
- Olive oil (for brushing)
- Salt and pepper (to taste)

Instructions:

1. Preheat your oven to the temperature specified on the pizza dough package or recipe (usually around 425°F or 220°C).
2. Roll out the pizza dough on a lightly floured surface to your desired thickness. Transfer the dough to a lightly greased baking sheet or pizza stone.
3. Brush the surface of the dough lightly with olive oil. This will help create a golden crust and prevent the toppings from making the crust soggy.
4. Spread the pizza sauce evenly over the dough, leaving a small border around the edges for the crust.
5. Sprinkle the shredded mozzarella cheese evenly over the sauce.
6. Arrange the sliced bell peppers, mushrooms, black olives, red onions, and cherry tomatoes evenly over the cheese.
7. Season the pizza with salt and pepper to taste.
8. Bake the pizza in the preheated oven for about 12-15 minutes, or until the crust is golden brown and the cheese is bubbly and melted.
9. Once done, remove the pizza from the oven and sprinkle the sliced fresh basil leaves over the top.
10. Let the pizza cool for a few minutes before slicing.
11. Slice the pizza, serve, and enjoy your delicious vegetarian feast!

Feel free to customize the toppings based on your preferences. You can add other veggies like spinach, artichoke hearts, or roasted garlic. You can also experiment with different cheeses or drizzle some balsamic glaze over the top for extra flavor.

Meat Lover's Pizza

Ingredients:

- 1 pizza dough (store-bought or homemade)
- 1/2 cup pizza sauce or marinara sauce
- 1 cup shredded mozzarella cheese
- 1/2 cup cooked and crumbled sausage
- 1/2 cup pepperoni slices
- 1/2 cup sliced ham or Canadian bacon
- 1/2 cup cooked and crumbled bacon
- 1/4 cup sliced black olives (optional)
- 1/4 cup sliced red onions (optional)
- 1/4 cup sliced bell peppers (optional)
- Olive oil (for brushing)

Instructions:

1. Preheat your oven to the temperature specified on the pizza dough package or recipe (usually around 425°F or 220°C).
2. Roll out the pizza dough on a lightly floured surface to your desired thickness. Transfer the dough to a lightly greased baking sheet or pizza stone.
3. Brush the surface of the dough lightly with olive oil. This will help create a golden crust and prevent the toppings from making the crust soggy.
4. Spread the pizza sauce evenly over the dough, leaving a small border around the edges for the crust.
5. Sprinkle the shredded mozzarella cheese evenly over the sauce.
6. Arrange the cooked and crumbled sausage, pepperoni slices, sliced ham or Canadian bacon, and cooked and crumbled bacon everly over the cheese.
7. If desired, add sliced black olives, red onions, or bell peppers on top of the meats
8. Bake the pizza in the preheated oven for about 12-15 minutes, or until the crust is golden brown and the cheese is bubbly and melted.
9. Once done, remove the pizza from the oven and let it cool for a few minutes before slicing.
10. Slice the pizza, serve, and enjoy your Meat Lover's Pizza!

Feel free to customize the toppings based on your preferences. You can add other meats like cooked ground beef, chicken, or Italian sausage. You can also experiment with different cheeses or add a sprinkle of dried oregano or red pepper flakes for extra flavor.

Buffalo Chicken Pizza

Ingredients:

For the buffalo chicken:

- 2 boneless, skinless chicken breasts
- Salt and pepper to taste
- 1/2 cup buffalo sauce (store-bought or homemade)
- 2 tablespoons unsalted butter, melted

For the pizza:

- 1 pizza dough (store-bought or homemade)
- 1/2 cup ranch or blue cheese dressing
- 1 cup shredded mozzarella cheese
- 1/4 cup crumbled blue cheese (optional)
- 2 green onions, thinly sliced
- Fresh cilantro or parsley leaves for garnish (optional)
- Extra buffalo sauce for drizzling (optional)

Instructions:

1. Preheat your oven to the temperature specified on the pizza dough package or recipe (usually around 425°F or 220°C).
2. Season the chicken breasts with salt and pepper. Grill or bake the chicken until cooked through, then shred the meat using two forks.
3. In a bowl, mix the shredded chicken with the buffalo sauce and melted butter until well coated.
4. Roll out the pizza dough on a lightly floured surface to your desired thickness. Transfer the dough to a lightly greased baking sheet or pizza stone.
5. Spread the ranch or blue cheese dressing evenly over the dough, leaving a small border around the edges for the crust.
6. Sprinkle the shredded mozzarella cheese over the dressing.
7. Distribute the buffalo chicken evenly over the cheese.
8. If desired, sprinkle crumbled blue cheese over the top for extra flavor.
9. Bake the pizza in the preheated oven for about 12-15 minutes, or until the crust is golden brown and the cheese is bubbly and melted.

10. Once done, remove the pizza from the oven and garnish with sliced green onions and fresh cilantro or parsley leaves.
11. If desired, drizzle extra buffalo sauce over the top for an added kick.
12. Let the pizza cool for a few minutes before slicing.
13. Slice the pizza, serve, and enjoy your delicious Buffalo Chicken Pizza!

Feel free to customize the toppings to your liking. You can add sliced red onions, diced celery, or jalapeños for extra flavor and crunch. Adjust the amount of buffalo sauce according to your preferred level of spiciness. Enjoy!

Four Cheese Pizza

Ingredients:

- 1 pizza dough (store-bought or homemade)
- 1/2 cup pizza sauce or marinara sauce
- 1 cup shredded mozzarella cheese
- 1/2 cup shredded cheddar cheese
- 1/2 cup shredded provolone cheese
- 1/2 cup crumbled feta cheese
- 2 cloves garlic, minced (optional)
- Fresh basil leaves, thinly sliced (optional)
- Red pepper flakes (optional)
- Olive oil (for brushing)

Instructions:

1. Preheat your oven to the temperature specified on the pizza dough package or recipe (usually around 425°F or 220°C).
2. Roll out the pizza dough on a lightly floured surface to your desired thickness. Transfer the dough to a lightly greased baking sheet or pizza stone.
3. Brush the surface of the dough lightly with olive oil. This will help create a golden crust and prevent the toppings from making the crust soggy.
4. Spread the pizza sauce evenly over the dough, leaving a small border around the edges for the crust.
5. Sprinkle the shredded mozzarella cheese evenly over the sauce.
6. Sprinkle the shredded cheddar cheese, provolone cheese, and crumbled feta cheese evenly over the mozzarella.
7. If desired, sprinkle minced garlic over the top for extra flavor.
8. Bake the pizza in the preheated oven for about 12-15 minutes, or until the crust is golden brown and the cheese is bubbly and melted.
9. Once done, remove the pizza from the oven and sprinkle thinly sliced fresh basil leaves and red pepper flakes over the top for added freshness and heat.
10. Let the pizza cool for a few minutes before slicing.
11. Slice the pizza, serve, and enjoy your indulgent Four Cheese Pizza!

Feel free to customize the cheeses to your liking. You can substitute any of the cheeses with your favorites, such as gouda, asiago, or fontina. Experiment with different combinations to find your perfect blend of cheesy goodness. Buon appetito!

Mediterranean Pizza

Ingredients:

For the pizza:

- 1 pizza dough (store-bought or homemade)
- 1/2 cup basil pesto sauce (store-bought or homemade)
- 1 cup shredded mozzarella cheese
- 1/2 cup marinated artichoke hearts, drained and chopped
- 1/2 cup sun-dried tomatoes, thinly sliced
- 1/4 cup sliced Kalamata olives
- 1/4 cup crumbled feta cheese
- Fresh basil leaves for garnish (optional)
- Olive oil (for brushing)

For the basil pesto sauce:

- 2 cups fresh basil leaves, packed
- 1/4 cup pine nuts or walnuts
- 2 cloves garlic, minced
- 1/2 cup grated Parmesan cheese
- 1/2 cup extra virgin olive oil
- Salt and pepper to taste

Instructions:

1. Preheat your oven to the temperature specified on the pizza dough package or recipe (usually around 425°F or 220°C).
2. To make the basil pesto sauce, combine the basil leaves, pine nuts or walnuts, minced garlic, and grated Parmesan cheese in a food processor. Pulse until the ingredients are finely chopped.
3. With the food processor running, slowly drizzle in the olive oil until the pesto is smooth and well combined. Season with salt and pepper to taste. Set aside.
4. Roll out the pizza dough on a lightly floured surface to your desired thickness. Transfer the dough to a lightly greased baking sheet or pizza stone.
5. Brush the surface of the dough lightly with olive oil. This will help create a golden crust and prevent the toppings from making the crust soggy.

6. Spread the basil pesto sauce evenly over the dough, leaving a small border around the edges for the crust.
7. Sprinkle the shredded mozzarella cheese evenly over the pesto sauce.
8. Arrange the chopped marinated artichoke hearts, thinly sliced sun-dried tomatoes, and sliced Kalamata olives evenly over the cheese.
9. Sprinkle crumbled feta cheese over the top of the pizza.
10. Bake the pizza in the preheated oven for about 12-15 minutes, or until the crust is golden brown and the cheese is bubbly and melted.
11. Once done, remove the pizza from the oven and garnish with fresh basil leaves, if desired.
12. Let the pizza cool for a few minutes before slicing.
13. Slice the pizza, serve, and enjoy your delicious Mediterranean Pizza!

Feel free to customize the toppings to your liking. You can add ingredients like roasted red peppers, artichoke hearts, spinach, or even grilled chicken for extra protein. Experiment with different cheeses and herbs to create your own unique Mediterranean flavor combination. Bon appétit!

White Pizza

Ingredients:

For the white sauce:

- 2 tablespoons unsalted butter
- 2 tablespoons all-purpose flour
- 1 cup whole milk
- 2 cloves garlic, minced
- 1/4 teaspoon dried thyme (optional)
- Salt and pepper to taste
- Pinch of nutmeg (optional)

For the pizza:

- 1 pizza dough (store-bought or homemade)
- 1 cup shredded mozzarella cheese
- 1/2 cup shredded fontina cheese
- 1/4 cup grated Parmesan cheese
- 2 tablespoons chopped fresh basil or parsley
- Crushed red pepper flakes (optional)
- Olive oil (for brushing)

Instructions:

1. Preheat your oven to the temperature specified on the pizza dough package or recipe (usually around 425°F or 220°C).
2. To make the white sauce, melt the butter in a saucepan over medium heat. Add the minced garlic and cook for 1-2 minutes, until fragrant.
3. Sprinkle the flour over the butter and garlic, stirring constantly to form a roux. Cook for 1-2 minutes, until the roux is lightly golden in color.
4. Slowly pour in the milk while whisking continuously to prevent lumps from forming. Cook the sauce, stirring frequently, until it thickens and coats the back of a spoon, about 5-7 minutes.
5. Stir in the dried thyme (if using), and season the sauce with salt, pepper, and a pinch of nutmeg to taste. Remove the sauce from the heat and set aside.

6. Roll out the pizza dough on a lightly floured surface to your desired thickness. Transfer the dough to a lightly greased baking sheet or pizza stone.
7. Brush the surface of the dough lightly with olive oil. This will help create a golden crust and prevent the toppings from making the crust soggy.
8. Spread the white sauce evenly over the dough, leaving a small border around the edges for the crust.
9. Sprinkle the shredded mozzarella cheese, shredded fontina cheese, and grated Parmesan cheese evenly over the sauce.
10. Bake the pizza in the preheated oven for about 12-15 minutes, or until the crust is golden brown and the cheese is bubbly and melted.
11. Once done, remove the pizza from the oven and sprinkle chopped fresh basil or parsley over the top. If desired, add a sprinkle of crushed red pepper flakes for a bit of heat.
12. Let the pizza cool for a few minutes before slicing.
13. Slice the pizza, serve, and enjoy your delicious White Pizza!

Feel free to customize the toppings to your liking. You can add ingredients like caramelized onions, roasted garlic, spinach, or cooked chicken for extra flavor and texture. Experiment with different cheeses and herbs to create your own signature white pizza. Enjoy!

Pesto Chicken Pizza

Ingredients:

For the pesto sauce:

- 2 cups fresh basil leaves, packed
- 1/4 cup pine nuts or walnuts
- 2 cloves garlic, minced
- 1/2 cup grated Parmesan cheese
- 1/2 cup extra virgin olive oil
- Salt and pepper to taste

For the pizza:

- 1 pizza dough (store-bought or homemade)
- 1 cup cooked chicken breast, shredded or diced
- 1/2 cup pesto sauce (store-bought or homemade)
- 1 cup shredded mozzarella cheese
- 1/4 cup grated Parmesan cheese
- Red pepper flakes (optional)
- Fresh basil leaves for garnish (optional)
- Olive oil (for brushing)

Instructions:

1. Preheat your oven to the temperature specified on the pizza dough package or recipe (usually around 425°F or 220°C).
2. To make the pesto sauce, combine the basil leaves, pine nuts or walnuts, minced garlic, and grated Parmesan cheese in a food processor. Pulse until the ingredients are finely chopped.
3. With the food processor running, slowly drizzle in the olive oil until the pesto is smooth and well combined. Season with salt and pepper to taste. Set aside.
4. Roll out the pizza dough on a lightly floured surface to your desired thickness. Transfer the dough to a lightly greased baking sheet or pizza stone.
5. Brush the surface of the dough lightly with olive oil. This will help create a golden crust and prevent the toppings from making the crust soggy.
6. Spread the pesto sauce evenly over the dough, leaving a small border around the edges for the crust.

7. Scatter the cooked chicken breast evenly over the pesto sauce.
8. Sprinkle the shredded mozzarella cheese and grated Parmesan cheese evenly over the chicken.
9. If desired, sprinkle red pepper flakes over the top for a bit of heat.
10. Bake the pizza in the preheated oven for about 12-15 minutes, or until the crust is golden brown and the cheese is bubbly and melted.
11. Once done, remove the pizza from the oven and garnish with fresh basil leaves, if desired.
12. Let the pizza cool for a few minutes before slicing.
13. Slice the pizza, serve, and enjoy your delicious Pesto Chicken Pizza!

Feel free to customize the toppings to your liking. You can add ingredients like sliced cherry tomatoes, roasted red peppers, or black olives for extra flavor and texture. Experiment with different cheeses and herbs to create your own unique pesto chicken pizza. Enjoy!

Spinach and Feta Pizza

Ingredients:

- 1 pizza dough (store-bought or homemade)
- 1 cup pizza sauce or marinara sauce
- 2 cups fresh spinach leaves, washed and dried
- 1 cup crumbled feta cheese
- 1/4 cup sliced black olives
- 1/4 cup sliced red onion
- 2 cloves garlic, minced
- Crushed red pepper flakes (optional)
- Olive oil (for brushing)
- Salt and pepper to taste

Instructions:

1. Preheat your oven to the temperature specified on the pizza dough package or recipe (usually around 425°F or 220°C).
2. Roll out the pizza dough on a lightly floured surface to your desired thickness. Transfer the dough to a lightly greased baking sheet or pizza stone.
3. Brush the surface of the dough lightly with olive oil. This will help create a golden crust and prevent the toppings from making the crust soggy.
4. Spread the pizza sauce evenly over the dough, leaving a small border around the edges for the crust.
5. Scatter the fresh spinach leaves evenly over the sauce.
6. Sprinkle the crumbled feta cheese over the spinach.
7. Distribute the sliced black olives, sliced red onion, and minced garlic evenly over the top.
8. Season the pizza with salt, pepper, and crushed red pepper flakes (if using) to taste.
9. Bake the pizza in the preheated oven for about 12-15 minutes, or until the crust is golden brown and the cheese is bubbly and melted.
10. Once done, remove the pizza from the oven and let it cool for a few minutes before slicing.
11. Slice the pizza, serve, and enjoy your delicious Spinach and Feta Pizza!

Feel free to customize the toppings to your liking. You can add ingredients like sliced cherry tomatoes, roasted red peppers, or artichoke hearts for extra flavor and texture. Experiment with different cheeses or add a sprinkle of dried oregano or basil for extra seasoning. Enjoy!

Sausage and Mushroom Pizza

Ingredients:

- 1 pizza dough (store-bought or homemade)
- 1 cup pizza sauce or marinara sauce
- 1 cup shredded mozzarella cheese
- 1/2 cup cooked Italian sausage, crumbled
- 1/2 cup sliced mushrooms (cremini, button, or your favorite type)
- 2 cloves garlic, minced
- 1/4 cup sliced red onion (optional)
- 1 tablespoon olive oil
- Salt and pepper to taste
- Crushed red pepper flakes (optional)
- Fresh basil leaves for garnish (optional)

Instructions:

1. Preheat your oven to the temperature specified on the pizza dough package or recipe (usually around 425°F or 220°C).
2. In a skillet, heat the olive oil over medium heat. Add the sliced mushrooms and minced garlic. Cook, stirring occasionally, until the mushrooms are golden brown and the garlic is fragrant, about 5-7 minutes. Season with salt and pepper to taste. Set aside.
3. Roll out the pizza dough on a lightly floured surface to your desired thickness. Transfer the dough to a lightly greased baking sheet or pizza stone.
4. Spread the pizza sauce evenly over the dough, leaving a small border around the edges for the crust.
5. Sprinkle the shredded mozzarella cheese evenly over the sauce.
6. Scatter the crumbled Italian sausage and cooked mushrooms evenly over the cheese.
7. If using, add sliced red onion on top of the other toppings.
8. If desired, sprinkle crushed red pepper flakes over the top for a bit of heat.
9. Bake the pizza in the preheated oven for about 12-15 minutes, or until the crust is golden brown and the cheese is bubbly and melted.
10. Once done, remove the pizza from the oven and let it cool for a few minutes before slicing.
11. Garnish the pizza with fresh basil leaves, if desired.
12. Slice the pizza, serve, and enjoy your delicious Sausage and Mushroom Pizza!

Feel free to customize the toppings to your liking. You can use any type of sausage you prefer, such as sweet Italian sausage or spicy sausage. You can also add other ingredients like roasted red peppers, black olives, or caramelized onions for extra flavor. Enjoy!

Philly Cheesesteak Pizza

Ingredients:

For the pizza dough:

- 1 pizza dough (store-bought or homemade)

For the pizza toppings:

- 1 tablespoon olive oil
- 1 onion, thinly sliced
- 1 bell pepper, thinly sliced (green or red)
- 8 ounces thinly sliced steak (such as ribeye or sirloin)
- Salt and pepper to taste
- 1 cup shredded provolone cheese
- 1 cup shredded mozzarella cheese
- 2 tablespoons grated Parmesan cheese
- 1/4 cup sliced mushrooms (optional)
- 1/4 cup sliced cherry tomatoes (optional)
- 2 tablespoons chopped fresh parsley (optional)
- Salt and pepper to taste

For the sauce (optional):

- 1/4 cup mayonnaise
- 1 tablespoon ketchup
- 1 teaspoon Worcestershire sauce
- Salt and pepper to taste

Instructions:

1. Preheat your oven to the temperature specified on the pizza dough package or recipe (usually around 425°F or 220°C).
2. In a skillet, heat the olive oil over medium-high heat. Add the thinly sliced onions and bell peppers. Cook, stirring occasionally, until the vegetables are soft and caramelized, about 10-15 minutes. Remove from the skillet and set aside.
3. In the same skillet, add the thinly sliced steak. Season with salt and pepper to taste. Cook, stirring occasionally, until the steak is browned and cooked to your

desired level of doneness, about 5-7 minutes. Remove from the skillet and set aside.
4. If using, prepare the sauce by combining the mayonnaise, ketchup, Worcestershire sauce, salt, and pepper in a small bowl. Set aside.
5. Roll out the pizza dough on a lightly floured surface to your desired thickness. Transfer the dough to a lightly greased baking sheet or pizza stone.
6. If using the sauce, spread it evenly over the dough, leaving a small border around the edges for the crust.
7. Sprinkle half of the shredded provolone cheese and mozzarella cheese over the sauce (if using).
8. Spread the cooked onions, bell peppers, and steak evenly over the cheese.
9. If using, add the sliced mushrooms and cherry tomatoes on top of the other toppings.
10. Sprinkle the remaining shredded provolone cheese and mozzarella cheese over the toppings.
11. Bake the pizza in the preheated oven for about 12-15 minutes, or until the crust is golden brown and the cheese is bubbly and melted.
12. Once done, remove the pizza from the oven and sprinkle the grated Parmesan cheese and chopped parsley over the top.
13. Let the pizza cool for a few minutes before slicing.
14. Slice the pizza, serve, and enjoy your delicious Philly Cheesesteak Pizza!

Feel free to customize the toppings to your liking. You can add ingredients like sliced mushrooms, cherry tomatoes, or even jalapeños for extra flavor and heat. Enjoy!

Taco Pizza

Ingredients:

For the pizza dough:

- 1 pizza dough (store-bought or homemade)

For the taco meat:

- 1 tablespoon olive oil
- 1 pound ground beef or turkey
- 1 packet taco seasoning mix
- 1/4 cup water

For the pizza toppings:

- 1 cup refried beans
- 1 cup shredded Mexican blend cheese
- 1 cup diced tomatoes
- 1/2 cup sliced black olives
- 1/4 cup sliced jalapeños (optional)
- 1/4 cup chopped green onions
- 1/4 cup chopped fresh cilantro
- Sour cream and salsa for serving (optional)

Instructions:

1. Preheat your oven to the temperature specified on the pizza dough package or recipe (usually around 425°F or 220°C).
2. In a skillet, heat the olive oil over medium-high heat. Add the ground beef or turkey and cook, breaking it apart with a spoon, until browned and cooked through, about 5-7 minutes.
3. Drain any excess fat from the skillet. Add the taco seasoning mix and water to the skillet. Stir to combine, then simmer for 2-3 minutes until the mixture thickens slightly. Remove from heat and set aside.
4. Roll out the pizza dough on a lightly floured surface to your desired thickness. Transfer the dough to a lightly greased baking sheet or pizza stone.
5. Spread the refried beans evenly over the dough, leaving a small border around the edges for the crust.

6. Sprinkle half of the shredded Mexican blend cheese over the refried beans.
7. Spread the cooked taco meat evenly over the cheese.
8. Sprinkle the diced tomatoes, sliced black olives, and sliced jalapeños (if using) evenly over the taco meat.
9. Sprinkle the remaining shredded Mexican blend cheese over the toppings.
10. Bake the pizza in the preheated oven for about 12-15 minutes, or until the crust is golden brown and the cheese is bubbly and melted.
11. Once done, remove the pizza from the oven and sprinkle the chopped green onions and fresh cilantro over the top.
12. Slice the pizza, serve, and enjoy your delicious Taco Pizza!
13. Serve with sour cream and salsa on the side, if desired, for dipping or drizzling over the pizza slices.

Feel free to customize the toppings to your liking. You can add ingredients like sliced avocado, diced red onions, or shredded lettuce for extra freshness and flavor. Enjoy your taco pizza!

Bacon and Egg Breakfast Pizza

Ingredients:

For the pizza dough:

- 1 pizza dough (store-bought or homemade)

For the toppings:

- 6 slices bacon, cooked and crumbled
- 4 large eggs
- 1 cup shredded mozzarella cheese
- 1/4 cup grated Parmesan cheese
- 2 green onions, thinly sliced
- Salt and pepper to taste
- Fresh parsley or chives for garnish (optional)

Instructions:

1. Preheat your oven to the temperature specified on the pizza dough package or recipe (usually around 425°F or 220°C).
2. Roll out the pizza dough on a lightly floured surface to your desired thickness. Transfer the dough to a lightly greased baking sheet or pizza stone.
3. Spread the shredded mozzarella cheese evenly over the dough, leaving a small border around the edges for the crust.
4. Sprinkle the crumbled bacon evenly over the cheese.
5. Carefully crack the eggs onto the pizza, evenly spacing them apart. You can crack them directly onto the pizza or crack them into a small bowl first and then gently slide them onto the pizza.
6. Sprinkle the grated Parmesan cheese over the eggs. Season with salt and pepper to taste.
7. Bake the pizza in the preheated oven for about 10-12 minutes, or until the crust is golden brown, the cheese is bubbly, and the egg whites are set but the yolks are still slightly runny.
8. Once done, remove the pizza from the oven and let it cool for a few minutes.

9. Sprinkle the thinly sliced green onions over the top of the pizza. If desired, garnish with fresh parsley or chives for added freshness.
10. Slice the pizza, serve, and enjoy your delicious Bacon and Egg Breakfast Pizza!

Feel free to customize the toppings to your liking. You can add ingredients like diced tomatoes, sliced mushrooms, or cooked sausage for extra flavor and texture. Serve with hot sauce or salsa on the side for extra kick if desired. Enjoy your breakfast pizza!

Fig and Prosciutto Pizza

Ingredients:

For the pizza dough:

- 1 pizza dough (store-bought or homemade)

For the toppings:

- 1/2 cup fig jam or fig preserves
- 4 ounces thinly sliced prosciutto
- 1 cup shredded mozzarella cheese
- 1/4 cup crumbled goat cheese
- 1/4 cup chopped walnuts
- 1/4 cup arugula leaves
- Balsamic glaze for drizzling (optional)
- Olive oil for brushing

Instructions:

1. Preheat your oven to the temperature specified on the pizza dough package or recipe (usually around 425°F or 220°C).
2. Roll out the pizza dough on a lightly floured surface to your desired thickness. Transfer the dough to a lightly greased baking sheet or pizza stone.
3. Brush the surface of the dough lightly with olive oil. This will help create a golden crust and prevent the toppings from making the crust soggy.
4. Spread the fig jam or fig preserves evenly over the dough, leaving a small border around the edges for the crust.
5. Arrange the thinly sliced prosciutto evenly over the fig jam.
6. Sprinkle the shredded mozzarella cheese over the prosciutto.
7. Dot the top of the pizza with crumbled goat cheese.
8. Sprinkle the chopped walnuts over the cheese.
9. Bake the pizza in the preheated oven for about 12-15 minutes, or until the crust is golden brown and the cheese is bubbly and melted.
10. Once done, remove the pizza from the oven and let it cool for a few minutes.
11. Top the pizza with fresh arugula leaves.

12. If desired, drizzle balsamic glaze over the top of the pizza for extra flavor.
13. Slice the pizza, serve, and enjoy your delicious Fig and Prosciutto Pizza!

Feel free to customize the toppings to your liking. You can add ingredients like caramelized onions, sliced pears, or blue cheese for extra flavor and texture. Experiment with different cheeses or herbs to create your own unique variation of this delicious pizza. Enjoy!

Shrimp Scampi Pizza

Ingredients:

For the pizza dough:

- 1 pizza dough (store-bought or homemade)

For the shrimp scampi topping:

- 1 pound large shrimp, peeled and deveined
- 4 tablespoons unsalted butter
- 4 cloves garlic, minced
- 1/4 cup white wine (or chicken broth)
- 2 tablespoons lemon juice
- Salt and pepper to taste
- Pinch of red pepper flakes (optional)
- 1/4 cup chopped fresh parsley

For the pizza:

- 1 cup shredded mozzarella cheese
- 1/4 cup grated Parmesan cheese
- 1 tablespoon olive oil
- Fresh parsley for garnish (optional)
- Lemon wedges for serving (optional)

Instructions:

1. Preheat your oven to the temperature specified on the pizza dough package or recipe (usually around 425°F or 220°C).
2. In a large skillet, melt the butter over medium heat. Add the minced garlic and cook for 1-2 minutes, until fragrant.
3. Add the shrimp to the skillet and cook for 2-3 minutes, until they start to turn pink.
4. Pour in the white wine (or chicken broth) and lemon juice. Season with salt, pepper, and a pinch of red pepper flakes, if using. Cook for another 2-3 minutes, until the shrimp are cooked through and the sauce has slightly thickened.
5. Remove the skillet from the heat and stir in the chopped fresh parsley. Set aside.

6. Roll out the pizza dough on a lightly floured surface to your desired thickness. Transfer the dough to a lightly greased baking sheet or pizza stone.
7. Brush the surface of the dough lightly with olive oil.
8. Spread the cooked shrimp scampi mixture evenly over the dough, leaving a small border around the edges for the crust.
9. Sprinkle the shredded mozzarella cheese and grated Parmesan cheese evenly over the shrimp scampi.
10. Bake the pizza in the preheated oven for about 12-15 minutes, or until the crust is golden brown and the cheese is bubbly and melted.
11. Once done, remove the pizza from the oven and let it cool for a few minutes.
12. Garnish the pizza with fresh parsley and serve with lemon wedges on the side, if desired.
13. Slice the pizza, serve, and enjoy your delicious Shrimp Scampi Pizza!

Feel free to customize the toppings to your liking. You can add ingredients like sliced cherry tomatoes, chopped artichoke hearts, or spinach for extra flavor and texture. Experiment with different cheeses or herbs to create your own unique variation of this delicious pizza. Enjoy!

Artichoke and Olive Pizza

Ingredients:

For the pizza dough:

- 1 pizza dough (store-bought or homemade)

For the toppings:

- 1 cup pizza sauce or marinara sauce
- 1 cup shredded mozzarella cheese
- 1/2 cup marinated artichoke hearts, drained and chopped
- 1/4 cup sliced black olives
- 1/4 cup sliced green olives
- 1/4 cup sliced red onion (optional)
- 2 cloves garlic, minced
- 1 tablespoon olive oil
- Salt and pepper to taste
- Crushed red pepper flakes (optional)
- Fresh basil leaves for garnish (optional)

Instructions:

1. Preheat your oven to the temperature specified on the pizza dough package or recipe (usually around 425°F or 220°C).
2. Roll out the pizza dough on a lightly floured surface to your desired thickness. Transfer the dough to a lightly greased baking sheet or pizza stone.
3. Brush the surface of the dough lightly with olive oil. This will help create a golden crust and prevent the toppings from making the crust soggy.
4. Spread the pizza sauce evenly over the dough, leaving a small border around the edges for the crust.
5. Sprinkle the shredded mozzarella cheese evenly over the sauce.
6. Scatter the chopped marinated artichoke hearts, sliced black olives, sliced green olives, and sliced red onion (if using) evenly over the cheese.
7. Sprinkle minced garlic over the top of the pizza. Season with salt, pepper, and crushed red pepper flakes (if using) to taste.
8. Bake the pizza in the preheated oven for about 12-15 minutes, or until the crust is golden brown and the cheese is bubbly and melted.

9. Once done, remove the pizza from the oven and let it cool for a few minutes.
10. If desired, garnish the pizza with fresh basil leaves for added freshness and flavor.
11. Slice the pizza, serve, and enjoy your delicious Artichoke and Olive Pizza!

Feel free to customize the toppings to your liking. You can add ingredients like roasted red peppers, sun-dried tomatoes, or feta cheese for extra flavor and texture. Experiment with different cheeses or herbs to create your own unique variation of this delicious pizza. Enjoy!

BBQ Pulled Pork Pizza

Ingredients:

- Pizza dough (store-bought or homemade)
- BBQ sauce (choose your favorite)
- Cooked pulled pork (leftover homemade or store-bought)
- Red onion, thinly sliced
- Mozzarella cheese, shredded
- Fresh cilantro, chopped (optional)
- Olive oil
- Cornmeal (for dusting)

Instructions:

1. Preheat your oven to the temperature specified for your pizza dough (usually around 425°F or 220°C).
2. Roll out the pizza dough on a lightly floured surface. f you like a thin crust, roll it out thinner; for a thicker crust, leave it a bit thicker.
3. Sprinkle some cornmeal on a pizza peel or the back of a baking sheet. This will help prevent the pizza from sticking.
4. Transfer the rolled-out dough to the pizza peel or baking sheet.
5. Brush the dough with a thin layer of olive oil.
6. Spread a generous amount of BBQ sauce over the dough, leaving a small border around the edges for the crust.
7. Evenly distribute the cooked pulled pork over the BBQ sauce.
8. Scatter the thinly sliced red onions over the pulled pork.
9. Sprinkle a generous amount of shredded mozzarella cheese over the entire pizza.
10. If desired, sprinkle some chopped fresh cilantro over the top for added flavor.
11. Carefully transfer the pizza to the preheated oven and bake according to the dough's instructions or until the crust is golden brown and the cheese is melted and bubbly.
12. Once done, remove the pizza from the oven and let it cool for a minute or two before slicing.
13. Serve hot and enjoy the delicious BBQ pulled pork pizza!

Feel free to customize this recipe by adding your favorite toppings such as sliced bell peppers, jalapeños, or pineapple for a unique twist!

Chicken Alfredo Pizza

Ingredients:

- Pizza dough (store-bought or homemade)
- Alfredo sauce (store-bought or homemade)
- Cooked chicken breast, shredded or diced
- Mozzarella cheese, shredded
- Parmesan cheese, grated
- Fresh parsley, chopped (for garnish)
- Salt and black pepper
- Olive oil

Instructions:

1. Preheat your oven to the temperature specified for your pizza dough (usually around 425°F or 220°C).
2. Roll out the pizza dough on a lightly floured surface. If you like a thin crust, roll it out thinner; for a thicker crust, leave it a bit thicker.
3. Transfer the rolled-out dough to a pizza peel or the back of a baking sheet.
4. Brush the dough with a thin layer of olive oil.
5. Spread a layer of Alfredo sauce over the dough, leaving a small border around the edges for the crust.
6. Sprinkle a layer of shredded mozzarella cheese over the Alfredo sauce.
7. Distribute the cooked chicken breast evenly over the cheese.
8. Season with a pinch of salt and black pepper.
9. Sprinkle a layer of grated Parmesan cheese over the chicken.
10. Transfer the pizza to the preheated oven and bake according to the dough's instructions or until the crust is golden brown and the cheese is melted and bubbly.
11. Once done, remove the pizza from the oven and let it cool for a minute or two before slicing.
12. Garnish with chopped fresh parsley for a pop of color and flavor.
13. Serve hot and enjoy your delicious Chicken Alfredo pizza!

You can also add additional toppings such as sautéed mushrooms, spinach, or sun-dried tomatoes to customize your pizza to your liking.

Greek Pizza

Ingredients:

- Pizza dough (store-bought or homemade)
- Olive oil
- Tomato sauce or crushed tomatoes
- Mozzarella cheese, shredded
- Feta cheese, crumbled
- Kalamata olives, pitted and sliced
- Red onion, thinly sliced
- Fresh spinach leaves
- Cherry tomatoes, halved
- Fresh oregano leaves (or dried oregano)
- Salt and black pepper

Instructions:

1. Preheat your oven to the temperature specified for your pizza dough (usually around 425°F or 220°C).
2. Roll out the pizza dough on a lightly floured surface. If you like a thin crust, roll it out thinner; for a thicker crust, leave it a bit thicker.
3. Transfer the rolled-out dough to a pizza peel or the back of a baking sheet.
4. Brush the dough with a thin layer of olive oil.
5. Spread a layer of tomato sauce or crushed tomatoes over the dough, leaving a small border around the edges for the crust.
6. Sprinkle a layer of shredded mozzarella cheese over the sauce.
7. Scatter crumbled feta cheese over the mozzarella.
8. Distribute sliced Kalamata olives, thinly sliced red onion, halved cherry tomatoes, and fresh spinach leaves evenly over the cheese.
9. Season with salt, black pepper, and fresh oregano leaves (or dried oregano) to taste.
10. Transfer the pizza to the preheated oven and bake according to the dough's instructions or until the crust is golden brown and the cheese is melted and bubbly.
11. Once done, remove the pizza from the oven and let it cool for a minute or two before slicing.
12. Serve hot and enjoy your delicious Greek pizza!

Feel free to customize your Greek pizza by adding other traditional Mediterranean ingredients such as artichoke hearts, roasted red peppers, or even a drizzle of tzatziki sauce for extra flavor.

Caprese Pizza

Ingredients:

- Pizza dough (store-bought or homemade)
- Olive oil
- Tomato sauce or crushed tomatoes (optional)
- Fresh tomatoes, thinly sliced
- Fresh mozzarella cheese, sliced or torn into pieces
- Fresh basil leaves
- Balsamic glaze (optional)
- Salt and black pepper

Instructions:

1. Preheat your oven to the temperature specified for your pizza dough (usually around 425°F or 220°C).
2. Roll out the pizza dough on a lightly floured surface. If you like a thin crust, roll it out thinner; for a thicker crust, leave it a bit thicker.
3. Transfer the rolled-out dough to a pizza peel or the back of a baking sheet.
4. Brush the dough with a thin layer of olive oil. If desired, you can spread a thin layer of tomato sauce or crushed tomatoes over the dough, leaving a small border around the edges for the crust.
5. Arrange the thinly sliced fresh tomatoes evenly over the sauce or olive oil.
6. Place slices or torn pieces of fresh mozzarella cheese on top of the tomatoes.
7. Tear fresh basil leaves and scatter them over the pizza.
8. Season with a pinch of salt and black pepper to taste.
9. Drizzle a balsamic glaze over the pizza for added flavor, if desired.
10. Transfer the pizza to the preheated oven and bake according to the dough's instructions or until the crust is golden brown and the cheese is melted and bubbly.
11. Once done, remove the pizza from the oven and let it cool for a minute or two before slicing.
12. Serve hot and enjoy your delicious Caprese pizza!

Caprese pizza is best enjoyed fresh out of the oven when the flavors are at their peak.

It's a perfect choice for a light and refreshing meal or as an appetizer for a gathering.

Italian Sausage and Peppers Pizza

Ingredients:

- Pizza dough (store-bought or homemade)
- Olive oil
- Tomato sauce or crushed tomatoes
- Italian sausage, cooked and sliced
- Bell peppers (red, green, and/or yellow), thinly sliced
- Onion, thinly sliced
- Mozzarella cheese, shredded
- Parmesan cheese, grated
- Italian seasoning (or a mixture of dried oregano, basil, and thyme)
- Red pepper flakes (optional, for added heat)
- Salt and black pepper

Instructions:

1. Preheat your oven to the temperature specified for your pizza dough (usually around 425°F or 220°C).
2. Roll out the pizza dough on a lightly floured surface. If you like a thin crust, roll it out thinner; for a thicker crust, leave it a bit thicker.
3. Transfer the rolled-out dough to a pizza peel or the back of a baking sheet.
4. Brush the dough with a thin layer of olive oil.
5. Spread a layer of tomato sauce or crushed tomatoes over the dough, leaving a small border around the edges for the crust.
6. Evenly distribute the cooked Italian sausage slices over the sauce.
7. Scatter thinly sliced bell peppers and onions over the sausage.
8. Sprinkle a generous amount of shredded mozzarella cheese over the pizza.
9. Grate some Parmesan cheese over the mozzarella.
10. Sprinkle Italian seasoning (or your preferred combination of dried herbs) over the pizza, along with red pepper flakes if you like it spicy.
11. Season with salt and black pepper to taste.
12. Transfer the pizza to the preheated oven and bake according to the dough's instructions or until the crust is golden brown and the cheese is melted and bubbly.
13. Once done, remove the pizza from the oven and let it cool for a minute or two before slicing.
14. Serve hot and enjoy your delicious Italian sausage and peppers pizza!

This pizza is perfect for gatherings or family dinners, and you can customize it further by adding other toppings like mushrooms, olives, or even a drizzle of balsamic glaze for extra flavor.

Roasted Vegetable Pizza

Ingredients:

- Pizza dough (store-bought or homemade)
- Olive oil
- Tomato sauce or pesto
- Assorted vegetables, such as:
    - Bell peppers (red, yellow, green), thinly sliced
    - Zucchini, thinly sliced
    - Eggplant, thinly sliced
    - Red onion, thinly sliced
    - Cherry tomatoes, halved
    - Mushrooms, sliced
    - Any other vegetables of your choice
- Mozzarella cheese, shredded
- Parmesan cheese, grated
- Fresh basil leaves, torn
- Salt and black pepper

Instructions:

1. Preheat your oven to the temperature specified for your pizza dough (usually around 425°F or 220°C).
2. Toss the assorted vegetables with olive oil, salt, and black pepper in a bowl until they are evenly coated.
3. Spread the vegetables in a single layer on a baking sheet and roast them in the preheated oven for about 15-20 minutes, or until they are tender and slightly caramelized. Remove from the oven and set aside.
4. Roll out the pizza dough on a lightly floured surface. If you like a thin crust, roll it out thinner; for a thicker crust, leave it a bit thicker.
5. Transfer the rolled-out dough to a pizza peel or the back of a baking sheet.
6. Brush the dough with a thin layer of olive oil. Alternatively, you can spread a layer of tomato sauce or pesto over the dough, leaving a small border around the edges for the crust.
7. Sprinkle a layer of shredded mozzarella cheese over the sauce or olive oil.
8. Arrange the roasted vegetables evenly over the cheese.
9. Sprinkle grated Parmesan cheese over the vegetables.

10. Transfer the pizza to the preheated oven and bake according to the dough's instructions or until the crust is golden brown and the cheese is melted and bubbly.
11. Once done, remove the pizza from the oven and let it cool for a minute or two before slicing.
12. Garnish with torn fresh basil leaves for a pop of color and flavor.
13. Serve hot and enjoy your delicious roasted vegetable pizza!

Feel free to customize this pizza with your favorite vegetables and herbs. It's a great way to use up leftover vegetables and create a healthy and flavorful meal.

Taco Supreme Pizza

Ingredients:

For the pizza dough:

- Pizza dough (store-bought or homemade)

For the toppings:

- 1 pound (450g) ground beef or turkey
- 1 packet (about 1 ounce or 28g) taco seasoning mix
- 1/2 cup (120ml) water
- 1 cup (240ml) refried beans
- 1 cup (240ml) salsa
- 1 cup (240ml) shredded Mexican blend cheese (or a combination of cheddar and Monterey Jack)
- 1 cup (240ml) shredded lettuce
- 1 large tomato, diced
- 1/2 cup (120ml) sliced black olives
- 1/4 cup (60ml) diced red onion
- Sour cream (for garnish)
- Fresh cilantro, chopped (for garnish)
- Sliced jalapeños (optional, for extra heat)

Instructions:

1. Preheat your oven to the temperature specified for your pizza dough (usually around 425°F or 220°C).
2. In a skillet over medium heat, cook the ground beef or turkey until it's browned and crumbled. Drain any excess fat.
3. Add the taco seasoning mix and water to the skillet with the cooked meat. Stir well to combine and simmer for a few minutes until the mixture thickens slightly. Remove from heat and set aside.
4. Roll out the pizza dough on a lightly floured surface to your desired thickness.
5. Transfer the rolled-out dough to a pizza pan or baking sheet.

6. Spread a layer of refried beans over the pizza dough, leaving a small border around the edges for the crust.
7. Spread the salsa evenly over the refried beans.
8. Sprinkle the cooked taco meat mixture over the salsa.
9. Sprinkle the shredded cheese over the taco meat.
10. Place the pizza in the preheated oven and bake according to the dough's instructions or until the crust is golden brown and the cheese is melted and bubbly.
11. Once the pizza is done baking, remove it from the oven and let it cool for a minute or two.
12. Top the pizza with shredded lettuce, diced tomatoes, sliced black olives, diced red onion, and any other desired toppings.
13. Drizzle with sour cream and sprinkle with chopped fresh cilantro. Add sliced jalapeños if you like it spicy.
14. Slice the pizza, serve hot, and enjoy your Taco Supreme Pizza!

Feel free to customize this pizza with your favorite taco toppings, such as diced avocado, corn kernels, or chopped bell peppers. It's a fun and flavorful twist on traditional pizza that's sure to be a hit with taco lovers!

Bacon Cheeseburger Pizza

Ingredients:

For the pizza dough:

- Pizza dough (store-bought or homemade)

For the toppings:

- 8 slices of bacon, cooked until crispy and crumbled
- 1/2 pound (225g) ground beef
- 1/2 cup (120ml) ketchup
- 2 tablespoons (30ml) mustard
- 1 cup (240ml) shredded mozzarella cheese
- 1 cup (240ml) shredded cheddar cheese
- 1/4 cup (60ml) diced red onion
- Pickles, sliced
- Lettuce, shredded
- Tomato, diced
- Sesame seeds (optional, for garnish)

Instructions:

1. Preheat your oven to the temperature specified for your pizza dough (usually around 425°F or 220°C).
2. In a skillet over medium heat, cook the ground beef until it's browned and crumbled. Drain any excess fat.
3. In a small bowl, mix together the ketchup and mustard to create the pizza sauce.
4. Roll out the pizza dough on a lightly floured surface to your desired thickness.
5. Transfer the rolled-out dough to a pizza pan or baking sheet.
6. Spread a layer of the ketchup-mustard sauce over the pizza dough, leaving a small border around the edges for the crust.
7. Sprinkle the cooked ground beef evenly over the sauce.
8. Sprinkle the shredded mozzarella and cheddar cheeses over the ground beef.
9. Sprinkle the crumbled bacon and diced red onion over the cheese.

10. Place the pizza in the preheated oven and bake according to the dough's instructions or until the crust is golden brown and the cheese is melted and bubbly.
11. Once the pizza is done baking, remove it from the oven and let it cool for a minute or two.
12. Top the pizza with sliced pickles, shredded lettuce, and diced tomatoes.
13. If desired, sprinkle sesame seeds over the top for added flavor and texture.
14. Slice the pizza, serve hot, and enjoy your Bacon Cheeseburger Pizza!

Feel free to customize this pizza with your favorite burger toppings, such as sliced onions, mushrooms, or even a drizzle of barbecue sauce. It's a tasty twist on traditional pizza that's sure to satisfy your cravings for both bacon cheeseburgers and pizza!

Buffalo Cauliflower Pizza

Ingredients:

For the pizza dough:

- Pizza dough (store-bought or homemade)

For the buffalo cauliflower:

- 1 medium head of cauliflower, cut into florets
- 1/2 cup (120ml) buffalo sauce
- 2 tablespoons (30g) unsalted butter, melted
- 1 tablespoon (15ml) olive oil
- 1/2 teaspoon garlic powder
- Salt and pepper, to taste

For the toppings:

- 1/2 cup (120ml) buffalo sauce
- 1 cup (240ml) shredded mozzarella cheese
- 1/4 cup (60ml) crumbled blue cheese (optional)
- Green onions, thinly sliced (for garnish)
- Ranch or blue cheese dressing (for serving)

Instructions:

1. Preheat your oven to the temperature specified for your pizza dough (usually around 425°F or 220°C).
2. Toss the cauliflower florets with olive oil, garlic powder, salt, and pepper in a large bowl until evenly coated.
3. Spread the cauliflower florets in a single layer on a baking sheet lined with parchment paper. Bake in the preheated oven for about 20-25 minutes, or until the cauliflower is tender and slightly golden brown.
4. In a separate bowl, mix together the buffalo sauce and melted butter.

5. Once the cauliflower is done baking, transfer it to a large bowl and pour the buffalo sauce mixture over it. Toss until the cauliflower is evenly coated in the sauce.
6. Roll out the pizza dough on a lightly floured surface to your desired thickness.
7. Transfer the rolled-out dough to a pizza pan or baking sheet.
8. Spread a layer of buffalo sauce over the pizza dough, leaving a small border around the edges for the crust.
9. Sprinkle the shredded mozzarella cheese over the buffalo sauce.
10. Arrange the buffalo cauliflower evenly over the cheese.
11. If using, sprinkle crumbled blue cheese over the top.
12. Place the pizza in the preheated oven and bake according to the dough's instructions or until the crust is golden brown and the cheese is melted and bubbly.
13. Once the pizza is done baking, remove it from the oven and let it cool for a minute or two.
14. Garnish with thinly sliced green onions and serve with ranch or blue cheese dressing on the side.
15. Slice the pizza, serve hot, and enjoy your Buffalo Cauliflower Pizza!

Feel free to customize this pizza with additional toppings such as sliced red onions, diced celery, or chopped cilantro. It's a delicious and satisfying vegetarian option that packs all the flavor of buffalo wings into a healthier pizza alternative.

Chicken Tikka Masala Pizza

Ingredients:

For the pizza dough:

- Pizza dough (store-bought or homemade)

For the chicken tikka masala:

- 1 pound (450g) boneless, skinless chicken breasts, cut into bite-sized pieces
- 1 cup (240g) plain yogurt
- 2 tablespoons (30ml) lemon juice
- 2 cloves garlic, minced
- 1 tablespoon (15g) grated fresh ginger
- 2 tablespoons (30ml) vegetable oil
- 2 tablespoons (30g) garam masala
- 1 teaspoon ground cumin
- 1 teaspoon ground coriander
- 1 teaspoon paprika
- Salt and black pepper, to taste

For the pizza:

- 1 cup (240g) tomato sauce or pizza sauce
- 1 cup (240g) shredded mozzarella cheese
- 1/4 cup (60g) diced red onion
- Fresh cilantro leaves, chopped (for garnish)
- Naan bread or flatbread (optional, for crust variation)

Instructions:

1. Preheat your oven to the temperature specified for your pizza dough (usually around 425°F or 220°C).
2. In a large bowl, combine the yogurt, lemon juice, minced garlic, grated ginger, vegetable oil, garam masala, ground cumin, ground coriander, paprika, salt, and black pepper. Mix well.

3. Add the chicken pieces to the marinade and toss until evenly coated. Cover and refrigerate for at least 1 hour, or overnight for best results.
4. Heat a grill pan or skillet over medium-high heat. Cook the marinated chicken pieces until they are cooked through and slightly charred, about 6-8 minutes per side. Remove from heat and set aside.
5. Roll out the pizza dough on a lightly floured surface to your desired thickness.
6. Transfer the rolled-out dough to a pizza pan or baking sheet. If using naan bread or flatbread as the crust, place it directly on the pan.
7. Spread a layer of tomato sauce or pizza sauce over the pizza dough or naan bread, leaving a small border around the edges for the crust.
8. Sprinkle the shredded mozzarella cheese over the sauce.
9. Arrange the cooked chicken tikka masala pieces evenly over the cheese.
10. Sprinkle diced red onion over the chicken.
11. Place the pizza in the preheated oven and bake according to the dough's instructions or until the crust is golden brown and the cheese is melted and bubbly.
12. Once the pizza is done baking, remove it from the oven and let it cool for a minute or two.
13. Garnish with chopped fresh cilantro leaves.
14. Slice the pizza, serve hot, and enjoy your Chicken Tikka Masala Pizza!

This fusion pizza is a delicious way to enjoy the flavors of Indian cuisine in a fun and creative way. Feel free to customize it with additional toppings such as sliced bell peppers, diced tomatoes, or a drizzle of yogurt sauce for extra flavor.

Macaroni and Cheese Pizza

Ingredients:

For the pizza dough:

- Pizza dough (store-bought or homemade)

For the macaroni and cheese:

- 8 ounces (225g) elbow macaroni
- 2 tablespoons (30g) unsalted butter
- 2 tablespoons (15g) all-purpose flour
- 1 1/2 cups (360ml) whole milk
- 2 cups (200g) shredded cheddar cheese
- Salt and black pepper, to taste
- Pinch of paprika (optional)
- Pinch of nutmeg (optional)

For the toppings:

- 1 cup (240g) prepared macaroni and cheese
- 1 cup (240g) shredded mozzarella cheese
- 1/4 cup (60g) grated Parmesan cheese
- Cooked bacon, crumbled (optional)
- Sliced green onions or chives (optional)

Instructions:

1. Preheat your oven to the temperature specified for your pizza dough (usually around 425°F or 220°C).
2. Cook the elbow macaroni according to the package instructions until al dente. Drain and set aside.
3. In a medium saucepan, melt the butter over medium heat. Add the flour and whisk continuously for 1-2 minutes to create a roux.
4. Gradually pour in the milk while whisking constantly to avoid lumps. Continue cooking until the mixture thickens, about 5 minutes.
5. Reduce the heat to low and stir in the shredded cheddar cheese until melted and smooth. Season with salt, black pepper, paprika, and nutmeg, if using.

6. Add the cooked macaroni to the cheese sauce and stir until the macaroni is evenly coated.
7. Roll out the pizza dough on a lightly floured surface to your desired thickness.
8. Transfer the rolled-out dough to a pizza pan or baking sheet.
9. Spread a layer of prepared macaroni and cheese over the pizza dough, leaving a small border around the edges for the crust.
10. Sprinkle shredded mozzarella cheese over the macaroni and cheese layer.
11. Sprinkle grated Parmesan cheese over the mozzarella.
12. If desired, sprinkle crumbled cooked bacon over the cheese.
13. Place the pizza in the preheated oven and bake according to the dough's instructions or until the crust is golden brown and the cheese is melted and bubbly.
14. Once the pizza is done baking, remove it from the oven and let it cool for a minute or two.
15. Garnish with sliced green onions or chives, if using.
16. Slice the pizza, serve hot, and enjoy your Macaroni and Cheese Pizza!

This pizza is a fun and indulgent twist on traditional macaroni and cheese, perfect for a cozy night in or a family dinner. Feel free to customize it with additional toppings such as diced tomatoes, caramelized onions, or jalapeños for extra flavor.

Ratatouille Pizza

Ingredients:

For the pizza dough:

- Pizza dough (store-bought or homemade)

For the ratatouille topping:

- 1 small eggplant, diced
- 1 small zucchini, diced
- 1 small yellow squash, diced
- 1 bell pepper, diced
- 1 onion, diced
- 2 cloves garlic, minced
- 2 tablespoons (30ml) olive oil
- 1 can (14 ounces or 400g) diced tomatoes
- 1 teaspoon dried thyme
- 1 teaspoon dried oregano
- Salt and black pepper, to taste

For assembling the pizza:

- 1 cup (240g) shredded mozzarella cheese
- 1/4 cup (60g) grated Parmesan cheese
- Fresh basil leaves, chopped (for garnish)
- Red pepper flakes (optional, for added heat)

Instructions:

1. Preheat your oven to the temperature specified for your pizza dough (usually around 425°F or 220°C).
2. Heat olive oil in a large skillet over medium heat. Add the diced eggplant, zucchini, yellow squash, bell pepper, onion, and minced garlic. Cook, stirring occasionally, until the vegetables are softened, about 8-10 minutes.
3. Stir in the diced tomatoes (with their juices), dried thyme, dried oregano, salt, and black pepper. Simmer for an additional 5-7 minutes, until the flavors have melded together and the mixture has thickened slightly. Remove from heat and set aside.
4. Roll out the pizza dough on a lightly floured surface to your desired thickness.

5. Transfer the rolled-out dough to a pizza pan or baking sheet.
6. Spread a layer of the ratatouille mixture over the pizza dough, leaving a small border around the edges for the crust.
7. Sprinkle shredded mozzarella cheese over the ratatouille mixture.
8. Sprinkle grated Parmesan cheese over the mozzarella.
9. If desired, sprinkle red pepper flakes over the cheese for added heat.
10. Place the pizza in the preheated oven and bake according to the dough's instructions or until the crust is golden brown and the cheese is melted and bubbly.
11. Once the pizza is done baking, remove it from the oven and let it cool for a minute or two.
12. Garnish with chopped fresh basil leaves.
13. Slice the pizza, serve hot, and enjoy your Ratatouille Pizza!

This pizza is a flavorful and vegetarian-friendly option that showcases the delicious flavors of ratatouille in a new and creative way. Feel free to customize it with additional toppings such as sliced olives, artichoke hearts, or sun-dried tomatoes for extra flavor.

Breakfast Burrito Pizza

Ingredients:

For the pizza dough:

- Pizza dough (store-bought or homemade)

For the toppings:

- 6 large eggs
- 1/4 cup (60ml) milk
- Salt and black pepper, to taste
- 1 tablespoon (15ml) vegetable oil
- 4 ounces (115g) breakfast sausage or bacon, cooked and crumbled
- 1 cup (240ml) shredded cheddar cheese
- 1/2 cup (120ml) salsa
- 1/4 cup (60ml) chopped green onions or chives
- 1/4 cup (60ml) chopped fresh cilantro (optional)
- Sour cream (optional, for serving)
- Sliced jalapeños (optional, for serving)

Instructions:

1. Preheat your oven to the temperature specified for your pizza dough (usually around 425°F or 220°C).
2. In a bowl, whisk together the eggs, milk, salt, and black pepper until well combined.
3. Heat the vegetable oil in a skillet over medium heat. Pour in the egg mixture and cook, stirring occasionally, until the eggs are scrambled and cooked through. Remove from heat and set aside.
4. Roll out the pizza dough on a lightly floured surface to your desired thickness.
5. Transfer the rolled-out dough to a pizza pan or baking sheet.
6. Spread the cooked scrambled eggs evenly over the pizza dough.
7. Sprinkle the cooked breakfast sausage or bacon over the scrambled eggs.
8. Sprinkle shredded cheddar cheese over the toppings.
9. Dollop salsa over the cheese.

10. Place the pizza in the preheated oven and bake according to the dough's instructions or until the crust is golden brown and the cheese is melted and bubbly.
11. Once the pizza is done baking, remove it from the oven and let it cool for a minute or two.
12. Garnish with chopped green onions or chives, and chopped fresh cilantro, if using.
13. Serve hot with optional toppings such as sour cream and sliced jalapeños.
14. Slice the pizza and enjoy your Breakfast Burrito Pizza!

This pizza is a delicious and satisfying option for breakfast or brunch. Feel free to customize it with additional toppings such as diced tomatoes, sliced avocado, or black beans for extra flavor.

Caramelized Onion and Gorgonzola Pizza

Ingredients:

For the pizza dough:

- Pizza dough (store-bought or homemade)

For the caramelized onions:

- 2 large onions, thinly sliced
- 2 tablespoons (30g) unsalted butter
- 1 tablespoon (15ml) olive oil
- Pinch of salt

For assembling the pizza:

- Caramelized onions (prepared as instructed above)
- 4 ounces (115g) gorgonzola cheese, crumbled
- 1/2 cup (120ml) shredded mozzarella cheese
- Fresh thyme leaves (optional, for garnish)
- Balsamic glaze (optional, for drizzling)

Instructions:

1. Preheat your oven to the temperature specified for your pizza dough (usually around 425°F or 220°C).
2. In a large skillet, heat the butter and olive oil over medium heat. Add the thinly sliced onions and a pinch of salt. Cook, stirring occasionally, until the onions are soft and golden brown, about 20-25 minutes. Remove from heat and set aside.
3. Roll out the pizza dough on a lightly floured surface to your desired thickness.
4. Transfer the rolled-out dough to a pizza pan or baking sheet.
5. Spread a layer of caramelized onions over the pizza dough, leaving a small border around the edges for the crust.
6. Sprinkle crumbled gorgonzola cheese over the caramelized onions.
7. Sprinkle shredded mozzarella cheese over the gorgonzola.
8. If desired, sprinkle fresh thyme leaves over the cheese.
9. Place the pizza in the preheated oven and bake according to the dough's instructions or until the crust is golden brown and the cheese is melted and bubbly.

10. Once the pizza is done baking, remove it from the oven and let it cool for a minute or two.
11. If desired, drizzle balsamic glaze over the top for added flavor.
12. Slice the pizza and serve hot.

This caramelized onion and gorgonzola pizza is a delightful combination of sweet and savory flavors. It's perfect for a cozy night in or as an appetizer for a dinner party. Enjoy!

Mushroom and Truffle Oil Pizza

Ingredients:

For the pizza dough:

- Pizza dough (store-bought or homemade)

For the toppings:

- 2 cups (about 225g) assorted mushrooms (such as cremini, shiitake, and oyster), thinly sliced
- 2 tablespoons (30ml) olive oil
- 2 cloves garlic, minced
- Salt and black pepper, to taste
- 1 cup (240ml) shredded mozzarella cheese
- 1/4 cup (60ml) grated Parmesan cheese
- 2 teaspoons (10ml) truffle oil
- Fresh parsley, chopped (for garnish)

Instructions:

1. Preheat your oven to the temperature specified for your pizza dough (usually around 425°F or 220°C).
2. In a skillet, heat the olive oil over medium heat. Add the minced garlic and cook for about 1 minute, until fragrant.
3. Add the sliced mushrooms to the skillet and sauté until they are tender and any liquid released has evaporated, about 5-7 minutes. Season with salt and black pepper to taste. Remove from heat and set aside.
4. Roll out the pizza dough on a lightly floured surface to your desired thickness.
5. Transfer the rolled-out dough to a pizza pan or baking sheet.
6. Sprinkle the shredded mozzarella cheese evenly over the pizza dough.
7. Spread the sautéed mushrooms over the cheese.
8. Sprinkle the grated Parmesan cheese over the mushrooms.
9. Drizzle the truffle oil over the pizza.

10. Place the pizza in the preheated oven and bake according to the dough's instructions or until the crust is golden brown and the cheese is melted and bubbly.
11. Once the pizza is done baking, remove it from the oven and let it cool for a minute or two.
12. Garnish with chopped fresh parsley for a pop of color and added flavor.
13. Slice the pizza and serve hot.

This mushroom and truffle oil pizza is a decadent treat that is sure to impress. Enjoy the rich and earthy flavors with a hint of truffle essence in every bite!

Thai Chicken Pizza

Ingredients:

For the pizza dough:

- Pizza dough (store-bought or homemade)

For the Thai chicken topping:

- 1 boneless, skinless chicken breast, thinly sliced
- 2 tablespoons (30ml) soy sauce
- 1 tablespoon (15ml) fish sauce
- 1 tablespoon (15ml) rice vinegar
- 1 tablespoon (15ml) honey
- 1 tablespoon (15ml) sriracha sauce (adjust to taste for spiciness)
- 1 clove garlic, minced
- 1 tablespoon (15ml) vegetable oil
- 1/2 cup (120ml) peanut sauce (store-bought or homemade)
- 1/2 cup (120ml) shredded mozzarella cheese
- 1/4 cup (60ml) shredded carrots
- 1/4 cup (60ml) sliced red bell pepper
- 1/4 cup (60ml) sliced red onion
- 2 tablespoons (30ml) chopped fresh cilantro
- Crushed peanuts (optional, for garnish)
- Lime wedges (optional, for serving)

Instructions:

1. Preheat your oven to the temperature specified for your pizza dough (usually around 425°F or 220°C).
2. In a bowl, whisk together the soy sauce, fish sauce, rice vinegar, honey, sriracha sauce, and minced garlic to make the marinade.
3. Add the thinly sliced chicken breast to the marinade and toss until evenly coated. Let it marinate for at least 15-20 minutes.
4. Heat the vegetable oil in a skillet over medium-high heat. Add the marinated chicken slices and cook until they are browned and cooked through, about 5-7 minutes. Remove from heat and set aside.
5. Roll out the pizza dough on a lightly floured surface to your desired thickness.

6. Transfer the rolled-out dough to a pizza pan or baking sheet.
7. Spread a layer of peanut sauce over the pizza dough, leaving a small border around the edges for the crust.
8. Sprinkle shredded mozzarella cheese over the peanut sauce.
9. Arrange the cooked chicken slices, shredded carrots, sliced red bell pepper, and sliced red onion evenly over the cheese.
10. Place the pizza in the preheated oven and bake according to the dough's instructions or until the crust is golden brown and the cheese is melted and bubbly.
11. Once the pizza is done baking, remove it from the oven and let it cool for a minute or two.
12. Garnish with chopped fresh cilantro and crushed peanuts, if desired.
13. Serve hot with lime wedges on the side for squeezing over the pizza.

This Thai chicken pizza is a flavorful and unique twist on traditional pizza, combining the bold and tangy flavors of Thai cuisine with the comfort of a classic pizza. Enjoy!

Smoked Salmon and Dill Pizza

Ingredients:

For the pizza dough:

- Pizza dough (store-bought or homemade)

For the toppings:

- 4 ounces (115g) smoked salmon, thinly sliced
- 1/4 cup (60g) cream cheese
- 1 tablespoon (15ml) lemon juice
- 1 tablespoon (15ml) capers, drained
- 1 tablespoon (15ml) chopped fresh dill
- 1/4 cup (60g) red onion, thinly sliced
- 1 tablespoon (15ml) olive oil
- Salt and black pepper, to taste
- Lemon wedges (for serving)

Instructions:

1. Preheat your oven to the temperature specified for your pizza dough (usually around 425°F or 220°C).
2. Roll out the pizza dough on a lightly floured surface to your desired thickness.
3. Transfer the rolled-out dough to a pizza pan or baking sheet.
4. In a small bowl, mix together the cream cheese and lemon juice until smooth and spreadable.
5. Spread the cream cheese mixture evenly over the pizza dough, leaving a small border around the edges for the crust.
6. Arrange the thinly sliced smoked salmon over the cream cheese mixture.
7. Sprinkle the drained capers and chopped fresh dill over the smoked salmon.
8. Scatter the thinly sliced red onion over the top.
9. Drizzle olive oil over the pizza and season with salt and black pepper to taste.
10. Place the pizza in the preheated oven and bake according to the dough's instructions or until the crust is golden brown and the toppings are heated through.

11. Once the pizza is done baking, remove it from the oven and let it cool for a minute or two.
12. Garnish with additional fresh dill, if desired, and serve hot with lemon wedges on the side for squeezing over the pizza.

This smoked salmon and dill pizza is a sophisticated and flavorful dish that's perfect for brunch, lunch, or a light dinner. Enjoy the combination of creamy cheese, smoky salmon, and aromatic dill on a crispy pizza crust!

Peking Duck Pizza

Ingredients:

For the pizza dough:

- Pizza dough (store-bought or homemade)

For the Peking duck topping:

- 1 Peking duck breast, thinly sliced (you can use store-bought roasted duck or roast your own)
- 2 tablespoons (30ml) hoisin sauce
- 1 tablespoon (15ml) soy sauce
- 1 tablespoon (15ml) honey
- 1 teaspoon sesame oil
- 1 teaspoon grated ginger
- 1 clove garlic, minced
- 1/4 cup (60ml) sliced green onions (scallions)
- 1/4 cup (60ml) shredded carrots
- 1/4 cup (60ml) sliced cucumber
- 1 tablespoon (15ml) sesame seeds
- Fresh cilantro leaves, for garnish

Instructions:

1. Preheat your oven to the temperature specified for your pizza dough (usually around 425°F or 220°C).
2. In a small bowl, mix together the hoisin sauce, soy sauce, honey, sesame oil, grated ginger, and minced garlic to make the sauce.
3. Roll out the pizza dough on a lightly floured surface to your desired thickness.
4. Transfer the rolled-out dough to a pizza pan or baking sheet.
5. Spread a thin layer of the sauce over the pizza dough, leaving a small border around the edges for the crust.
6. Arrange the thinly sliced Peking duck breast evenly over the sauce.
7. Sprinkle sliced green onions, shredded carrots, and sliced cucumber over the duck.
8. Drizzle any remaining sauce over the top of the pizza.
9. Sprinkle sesame seeds over the pizza.

10. Place the pizza in the preheated oven and bake according to the dough's instructions or until the crust is golden brown and the toppings are heated through.
11. Once the pizza is done baking, remove it from the oven and let it cool for a minute or two.
12. Garnish with fresh cilantro leaves.
13. Slice the pizza and serve hot.

This Peking duck pizza is a unique and flavorful dish that combines the rich flavors of Peking duck with the convenience of pizza. Enjoy the delicious fusion of Chinese and Italian cuisine!

Reuben Pizza

Ingredients:

For the pizza dough:

- Pizza dough (store-bought or homemade)

For the toppings:

- 1/2 cup (120ml) thousand island dressing
- 1 cup (150g) shredded Swiss cheese
- 1 cup (150g) shredded mozzarella cheese
- 1 cup (150g) thinly sliced corned beef
- 1 cup (150g) sauerkraut, drained
- 1/4 cup (60g) chopped dill pickles
- 1 tablespoon (15ml) olive oil
- Caraway seeds, for garnish (optional)

Instructions:

1. Preheat your oven to the temperature specified for your pizza dough (usually around 425°F or 220°C).
2. Roll out the pizza dough on a lightly floured surface to your desired thickness.
3. Transfer the rolled-out dough to a pizza pan or baking sheet.
4. Spread a layer of thousand island dressing over the pizza dough, leaving a small border around the edges for the crust.
5. Sprinkle shredded Swiss cheese and shredded mozzarella cheese evenly over the dressing.
6. Arrange the thinly sliced corned beef over the cheese.
7. Scatter sauerkraut evenly over the corned beef.
8. Sprinkle chopped dill pickles over the sauerkraut.
9. Drizzle olive oil over the top of the pizza.
10. If desired, sprinkle caraway seeds over the pizza for added flavor.
11. Place the pizza in the preheated oven and bake according to the dough's instructions or until the crust is golden brown and the cheese is melted and bubbly.

12. Once the pizza is done baking, remove it from the oven and let it cool for a minute or two.
13. Slice the pizza and serve hot.

This Reuben pizza is a delicious and satisfying dish that captures the flavors of the classic Reuben sandwich in a fun and creative way. Enjoy the combination of tangy sauerkraut, savory corned beef, and creamy thousand island dressing on a crispy pizza crust!

Chicken Shawarma Pizza

Ingredients:

For the pizza dough:

- Pizza dough (store-bought or homemade)

For the shawarma chicken:

- 1 pound (450g) boneless, skinless chicken breasts or thighs, thinly sliced
- 2 cloves garlic, minced
- 1 tablespoon (15ml) lemon juice
- 1 tablespoon (15ml) olive oil
- 1 teaspoon ground cumin
- 1 teaspoon paprika
- 1/2 teaspoon ground turmeric
- 1/2 teaspoon ground coriander
- 1/4 teaspoon ground cinnamon
- Salt and black pepper, to taste

For assembling the pizza:

- 1/2 cup (120ml) plain Greek yogurt
- 2 tablespoons (30ml) tahini
- 2 tablespoons (30ml) lemon juice
- 2 cloves garlic, minced
- Salt and black pepper, to taste
- 1 cup (150g) shredded mozzarella cheese
- 1/2 cup (75g) cherry tomatoes, halved
- 1/4 cup (40g) sliced red onion
- Fresh parsley, chopped (for garnish)
- Hot sauce or chili flakes (optional, for added heat)

Instructions:

1. Preheat your oven to the temperature specified for your pizza dough (usually around 425°F or 220°C).
2. In a bowl, combine the minced garlic, lemon juice, olive oil, ground cumin, paprika, turmeric, coriander, cinnamon, salt, and black pepper to make the marinade.
3. Add the thinly sliced chicken to the marinade and toss until evenly coated. Let it marinate for at least 30 minutes, or refrigerate for up to 4 hours for maximum flavor.
4. In a separate bowl, mix together the Greek yogurt, tahini, lemon juice, minced garlic, salt, and black pepper to make the sauce. Set aside.
5. Roll out the pizza dough on a lightly floured surface to your desired thickness.
6. Transfer the rolled-out dough to a pizza pan or baking sheet.
7. Spread a layer of the yogurt-tahini sauce over the pizza dough, leaving a small border around the edges for the crust.
8. Sprinkle shredded mozzarella cheese over the sauce.
9. Arrange the marinated chicken slices evenly over the cheese.
10. Scatter cherry tomato halves and sliced red onion over the chicken.
11. Drizzle any remaining marinade over the top of the pizza.
12. Place the pizza in the preheated oven and bake according to the dough's instructions or until the crust is golden brown and the cheese is melted and bubbly.
13. Once the pizza is done baking, remove it from the oven and let it cool for a minute or two.
14. Garnish with chopped fresh parsley and hot sauce or chili flakes, if desired.
15. Slice the pizza and serve hot.

This chicken shawarma pizza is a flavorful and satisfying dish that combines the bold spices of shawarma with the cheesy goodness of pizza. Enjoy the fusion of flavors and textures in every bite!

Spaghetti and Meatball Pizza

Ingredients:

For the pizza dough:

- Pizza dough (store-bought or homemade)

For the toppings:

- 1 cup (240g) marinara sauce
- 1 cup (150g) shredded mozzarella cheese
- 1/4 cup (20g) grated Parmesan cheese
- 6-8 cooked meatballs, sliced in half
- 1 cup (240g) cooked spaghetti
- 2 tablespoons (30ml) olive oil
- 2 cloves garlic, minced
- Salt and black pepper, to taste
- Fresh basil leaves, chopped (for garnish)

Instructions:

1. Preheat your oven to the temperature specified for your pizza dough (usually around 425°F or 220°C).
2. Roll out the pizza dough on a lightly floured surface to your desired thickness.
3. Transfer the rolled-out dough to a pizza pan or baking sheet.
4. In a small bowl, mix together the olive oil and minced garlic. Brush the garlic oil mixture evenly over the pizza dough.
5. Spread a layer of marinara sauce over the garlic oil-coated pizza dough, leaving a small border around the edges for the crust.
6. Sprinkle shredded mozzarella cheese evenly over the sauce.
7. Arrange the sliced meatballs over the cheese.
8. Distribute the cooked spaghetti evenly over the meatballs.
9. Sprinkle grated Parmesan cheese over the spaghetti.
10. Season with salt and black pepper to taste.
11. Place the pizza in the preheated oven and bake according to the dough's instructions or until the crust is golden brown and the cheese is melted and bubbly.

12. Once the pizza is done baking, remove it from the oven and let it cool for a minute or two.
13. Garnish with chopped fresh basil leaves.
14. Slice the pizza and serve hot.

This spaghetti and meatball pizza is a fun and delicious way to enjoy the flavors of two classic Italian dishes in one. Enjoy the cheesy goodness and savory meatballs on top of a crispy pizza crust!

Tandoori Paneer Pizza

Ingredients:

For the pizza dough:

- Pizza dough (store-bought or homemade)

For the tandoori paneer:

- 8 ounces (225g) paneer, cut into cubes
- 1/2 cup (120g) plain yogurt
- 2 tablespoons (30ml) lemon juice
- 2 cloves garlic, minced
- 1 tablespoon (15g) grated ginger
- 1 tablespoon (15ml) vegetable oil
- 1 tablespoon (15g) tandoori masala
- 1 teaspoon ground cumin
- 1 teaspoon ground coriander
- 1/2 teaspoon ground turmeric
- 1/4 teaspoon cayenne pepper (adjust to taste)
- Salt, to taste

For assembling the pizza:

- 1/2 cup (120g) tomato sauce or pizza sauce
- 1 cup (240g) shredded mozzarella cheese
- 1/4 cup (40g) sliced red onion
- 1/4 cup (40g) sliced bell peppers (any color)
- Fresh cilantro leaves, chopped (for garnish)
- Lemon wedges (for serving)

Instructions:

1. Preheat your oven to the temperature specified for your pizza dough (usually around 425°F or 220°C).

2. In a large bowl, combine the plain yogurt, lemon juice, minced garlic, grated ginger, vegetable oil, tandoori masala, ground cumin, ground coriander, ground turmeric, cayenne pepper, and salt. Mix well to form a marinade.
3. Add the paneer cubes to the marinade and toss until evenly coated. Cover and refrigerate for at least 30 minutes, or up to 4 hours for maximum flavor.
4. Roll out the pizza dough on a lightly floured surface to your desired thickness.
5. Transfer the rolled-out dough to a pizza pan or baking sheet.
6. Spread a layer of tomato sauce or pizza sauce over the pizza dough, leaving a small border around the edges for the crust.
7. Sprinkle shredded mozzarella cheese evenly over the sauce.
8. Arrange the marinated paneer cubes, sliced red onion, and sliced bell peppers evenly over the cheese.
9. Place the pizza in the preheated oven and bake according to the dough's instructions or until the crust is golden brown and the cheese is melted and bubbly.
10. Once the pizza is done baking, remove it from the oven and let it cool for a minute or two.
11. Garnish with chopped fresh cilantro leaves.
12. Serve hot with lemon wedges on the side for squeezing over the pizza.

This tandoori paneer pizza is a flavorful and satisfying dish that combines the aromatic spices of Indian cuisine with the cheesy goodness of pizza. Enjoy the fusion of flavors and textures in every bite!

BLT Pizza

Ingredients:

For the pizza dough:

- Pizza dough (store-bought or homemade)

For the toppings:

- 1/2 cup (120ml) mayonnaise
- 1 tablespoon (15ml) lemon juice
- 1 clove garlic, minced
- Salt and black pepper, to taste
- 1 cup (150g) shredded mozzarella cheese
- 1 cup (150g) cherry tomatoes, halved
- 4 slices bacon, cooked and crumbled
- 1 cup (30g) shredded iceberg lettuce
- 2 tablespoons (30ml) ranch dressing
- Fresh basil leaves, chopped (for garnish)

Instructions:

1. Preheat your oven to the temperature specified for your pizza dough (usually around 425°F or 220°C).
2. Roll out the pizza dough on a lightly floured surface to your desired thickness.
3. Transfer the rolled-out dough to a pizza pan or baking sheet.
4. In a small bowl, mix together the mayonnaise, lemon juice, minced garlic, salt, and black pepper to make a garlic aioli sauce.
5. Spread a thin layer of the garlic aioli sauce over the pizza dough, leaving a small border around the edges for the crust.
6. Sprinkle shredded mozzarella cheese evenly over the garlic aioli sauce.
7. Arrange the halved cherry tomatoes over the cheese.
8. Scatter the crumbled bacon evenly over the tomatoes.
9. Place the pizza in the preheated oven and bake according to the dough's instructions or until the crust is golden brown and the cheese is melted and bubbly.

10. Once the pizza is done baking, remove it from the oven and let it cool for a minute or two.
11. Toss the shredded iceberg lettuce with the ranch dressing until evenly coated.
12. Scatter the dressed lettuce over the cooked pizza.
13. Garnish with chopped fresh basil leaves.
14. Slice the pizza and serve hot.

This BLT pizza is a delicious and satisfying dish that captures the flavors of the classic BLT sandwich in a fun and creative way. Enjoy the combination of crispy bacon, juicy tomatoes, creamy aioli sauce, and fresh lettuce on top of a crispy pizza crust!

Eggplant Parmesan Pizza

Ingredients:

For the pizza dough:

- Pizza dough (store-bought or homemade)

For the toppings:

- 1 medium eggplant, sliced into 1/4-inch rounds
- Salt, for sweating the eggplant
- Olive oil, for brushing the eggplant
- 1 cup (240ml) marinara sauce
- 1 cup (150g) shredded mozzarella cheese
- 1/4 cup (20g) grated Parmesan cheese
- Fresh basil leaves, chopped (for garnish)
- Red pepper flakes (optional, for added heat)

Instructions:

1. Preheat your oven to the temperature specified for your pizza dough (usually around 425°F or 220°C).
2. Place the eggplant slices in a colander and sprinkle them with salt. Let them sit for about 30 minutes to draw out excess moisture. Rinse the eggplant slices under cold water and pat them dry with paper towels.
3. Brush the eggplant slices with olive oil on both sides. Place them on a baking sheet and roast in the preheated oven for about 15-20 minutes, or until they are tender and lightly browned. Remove from the oven and set aside.
4. Roll out the pizza dough on a lightly floured surface to your desired thickness.
5. Transfer the rolled-out dough to a pizza pan or baking sheet.
6. Spread a layer of marinara sauce over the pizza dough, leaving a small border around the edges for the crust.
7. Arrange the roasted eggplant slices evenly over the sauce.
8. Sprinkle shredded mozzarella cheese over the eggplant.
9. Sprinkle grated Parmesan cheese over the mozzarella.
10. If desired, sprinkle red pepper flakes over the cheese for added heat.

11. Place the pizza in the preheated oven and bake according to the dough's instructions or until the crust is golden brown and the cheese is melted and bubbly.
12. Once the pizza is done baking, remove it from the oven and let it cool for a minute or two.
13. Garnish with chopped fresh basil leaves.
14. Slice the pizza and serve hot.

This eggplant Parmesan pizza is a delicious and satisfying vegetarian option that combines the flavors of classic Eggplant Parmesan with the convenience of pizza. Enjoy the crispy eggplant slices, gooey cheese, and savory marinara sauce on top of a crispy pizza crust!

Pulled BBQ Jackfruit Pizza

Ingredients:

For the pizza dough:

- Pizza dough (store-bought or homemade)

For the pulled BBQ jackfruit:

- 1 can (20 ounces) young green jackfruit in brine or water, drained and rinsed
- 1/2 cup (120ml) barbecue sauce
- 1 tablespoon (15ml) olive oil
- 1/2 teaspoon smoked paprika
- 1/2 teaspoon garlic powder
- Salt and black pepper, to taste

For assembling the pizza:

- 1/2 cup (120ml) barbecue sauce
- 1 cup (150g) shredded mozzarella cheese
- 1/4 cup (30g) red onion, thinly sliced
- 2 tablespoons (30g) pickled jalapeños, sliced (optional)
- Fresh cilantro leaves, chopped (for garnish)

Instructions:

1. Preheat your oven to the temperature specified for your pizza dough (usually around 425°F or 220°C).
2. Drain and rinse the canned jackfruit. Pat the jackfruit dry with paper towels and shred it using your hands or a fork.
3. In a skillet, heat olive oil over medium heat. Add the shredded jackfruit, smoked paprika, garlic powder, salt, and black pepper. Cook for 5-7 minutes, stirring occasionally, until the jackfruit starts to brown and become tender.
4. Add barbecue sauce to the skillet and stir until the jackfruit is evenly coated. Cook for an additional 2-3 minutes, then remove from heat and set aside.
5. Roll out the pizza dough on a lightly floured surface to your desired thickness.

6. Transfer the rolled-out dough to a pizza pan or baking sheet.
7. Spread a layer of barbecue sauce over the pizza dough, leaving a small border around the edges for the crust.
8. Sprinkle shredded mozzarella cheese evenly over the barbecue sauce.
9. Spread the pulled BBQ jackfruit over the cheese.
10. Scatter thinly sliced red onion and pickled jalapeños (if using) over the jackfruit.
11. Place the pizza in the preheated oven and bake according to the dough's instructions or until the crust is golden brown and the cheese is melted and bubbly.
12. Once the pizza is done baking, remove it from the oven and let it cool for a minute or two.
13. Garnish with chopped fresh cilantro leaves.
14. Slice the pizza and serve hot.

This pulled BBQ jackfruit pizza is a delicious and satisfying vegetarian option that captures the smoky flavors of barbecue with the unique texture of jackfruit. Enjoy the combination of tangy barbecue sauce, gooey cheese, and flavorful toppings on a crispy pizza crust!

Crab Rangoon Pizza

Ingredients:

For the pizza dough:

- Pizza dough (store-bought or homemade)

For the toppings:

- 8 ounces (225g) imitation crab meat, shredded
- 1 cup (240g) cream cheese, softened
- 1/4 cup (60ml) mayonnaise
- 2 cloves garlic, minced
- 2 green onions, thinly sliced
- 1/4 cup (30g) shredded mozzarella cheese
- 1/4 cup (30g) shredded cheddar cheese
- 1 tablespoon (15ml) soy sauce
- 1 teaspoon Worcestershire sauce
- Salt and black pepper, to taste
- Sesame seeds, for garnish (optional)
- Sweet chili sauce, for serving (optional)

Instructions:

1. Preheat your oven to the temperature specified for your pizza dough (usually around 425°F or 220°C).
2. Roll out the pizza dough on a lightly floured surface to your desired thickness.
3. Transfer the rolled-out dough to a pizza pan or baking sheet.
4. In a mixing bowl, combine the softened cream cheese, mayonnaise, minced garlic, thinly sliced green onions, shredded mozzarella cheese, shredded cheddar cheese, soy sauce, Worcestershire sauce, salt, and black pepper. Mix until well combined.
5. Spread the cream cheese mixture evenly over the pizza dough, leaving a small border around the edges for the crust.
6. Sprinkle the shredded imitation crab meat over the cream cheese mixture.
7. If desired, sprinkle sesame seeds over the top for added texture and flavor.

8. Place the pizza in the preheated oven and bake according to the dough's instructions or until the crust is golden brown and the cheese is melted and bubbly.
9. Once the pizza is done baking, remove it from the oven and let it cool for a minute or two.
10. Drizzle sweet chili sauce over the pizza for added sweetness and spice, if desired.
11. Slice the pizza and serve hot.

This Crab Rangoon pizza is a unique and flavorful dish that combines the creamy richness of cream cheese with the savory taste of imitation crab meat, all on top of a crispy pizza crust. Enjoy the delicious fusion of flavors in every bite!

French Onion Soup Pizza

Ingredients:

For the pizza dough:

- Pizza dough (store-bought or homemade)

For the caramelized onions:

- 2 large onions, thinly sliced
- 2 tablespoons (30g) unsalted butter
- 1 tablespoon (15ml) olive oil
- 1 teaspoon granulated sugar
- Salt and black pepper, to taste

For assembling the pizza:

- 1 cup (240ml) beef broth
- 1 tablespoon (15ml) Worcestershire sauce
- 1 teaspoon balsamic vinegar
- 1 teaspoon dried thyme
- 1 cup (240g) shredded Gruyère cheese
- Fresh parsley, chopped (for garnish)
- Grated Parmesan cheese (for serving)

Instructions:

1. Preheat your oven to the temperature specified for your pizza dough (usually around 425°F or 220°C).
2. In a large skillet, melt the butter with the olive oil over medium heat. Add the thinly sliced onions and cook, stirring occasionally, until they start to soften, about 5 minutes.
3. Sprinkle the sugar over the onions and continue to cook, stirring occasionally, until the onions are golden brown and caramelized, about 20-25 minutes. Season with salt and black pepper to taste. Remove from heat and set aside.

4. In a small saucepan, combine the beef broth, Worcestershire sauce, balsamic vinegar, and dried thyme. Bring to a simmer and cook for about 5-10 minutes, until slightly reduced and flavorful. Remove from heat and set aside.
5. Roll out the pizza dough on a lightly floured surface to your desired thickness.
6. Transfer the rolled-out dough to a pizza pan or baking sheet.
7. Spread the caramelized onions evenly over the pizza dough, leaving a small border around the edges for the crust.
8. Sprinkle the shredded Gruyère cheese evenly over the caramelized onions.
9. Carefully pour the beef broth mixture over the pizza, distributing it evenly.
10. Place the pizza in the preheated oven and bake according to the dough's instructions or until the crust is golden brown and the cheese is melted and bubbly.
11. Once the pizza is done baking, remove it from the oven and let it cool for a minute or two.
12. Garnish with chopped fresh parsley and grated Parmesan cheese.
13. Slice the pizza and serve hot.

This French onion soup pizza is a delicious and comforting dish that combines the rich flavors of caramelized onions, beef broth, and Gruyère cheese on top of a crispy pizza crust. Enjoy the savory goodness of French onion soup in pizza form!

Jerk Chicken Pizza

Ingredients:

For the pizza dough:

- Pizza dough (store-bought or homemade)

For the jerk chicken:

- 2 boneless, skinless chicken breasts, cut into bite-sized pieces
- 2 tablespoons (30ml) olive oil
- 2 tablespoons (30ml) jerk seasoning
- 1 tablespoon (15ml) soy sauce
- 1 tablespoon (15ml) lime juice
- 2 cloves garlic, minced

For assembling the pizza:

- 1/2 cup (120ml) barbecue sauce
- 1 cup (150g) shredded mozzarella cheese
- 1/4 cup (40g) sliced red onion
- 1/4 cup (30g) sliced bell peppers (any color)
- Fresh cilantro leaves, chopped (for garnish)
- Pineapple chunks (optional, for topping)
- Red pepper flakes (optional, for added heat)

Instructions:

1. Preheat your oven to the temperature specified for your pizza dough (usually around 425°F or 220°C).
2. In a bowl, combine the olive oil, jerk seasoning, soy sauce, lime juice, and minced garlic to make a marinade.
3. Add the chicken pieces to the marinade and toss until evenly coated. Let it marinate for at least 30 minutes, or longer for more flavor.

4. Heat a skillet over medium-high heat. Add the marinated chicken pieces and cook until browned and cooked through, about 5-7 minutes. Remove from heat and set aside.
5. Roll out the pizza dough on a lightly floured surface to your desired thickness.
6. Transfer the rolled-out dough to a pizza pan or baking sheet.
7. Spread a layer of barbecue sauce over the pizza dough, leaving a small border around the edges for the crust.
8. Sprinkle shredded mozzarella cheese evenly over the barbecue sauce.
9. Arrange the cooked jerk chicken pieces, sliced red onion, and sliced bell peppers evenly over the cheese.
10. If desired, scatter pineapple chunks over the top for a sweet contrast to the spicy chicken.
11. Sprinkle red pepper flakes over the pizza for added heat, if desired.
12. Place the pizza in the preheated oven and bake according to the dough's instructions or until the crust is golden brown and the cheese is melted and bubbly.
13. Once the pizza is done baking, remove it from the oven and let it cool for a minute or two.
14. Garnish with chopped fresh cilantro leaves.
15. Slice the pizza and serve hot.

This jerk chicken pizza is a flavorful and satisfying dish that combines the bold and spicy flavors of jerk seasoning with the sweetness of barbecue sauce, all on top of a crispy pizza crust. Enjoy the delicious fusion of Caribbean and Italian cuisine!

Philly Cheesesteak Stuffed Crust Pizza

Ingredients:

For the pizza dough:

- Pizza dough (store-bought or homemade)

For the stuffed crust:

- String cheese sticks
- Olive oil

For the pizza toppings:

- 1 tablespoon (15ml) olive oil
- 1 onion, thinly sliced
- 1 green bell pepper, thinly sliced
- 8 ounces (225g) thinly sliced beef steak (such as ribeye or sirloin)
- Salt and black pepper, to taste
- 1 cup (240g) shredded provolone cheese
- 1/4 cup (30g) shredded mozzarella cheese
- 1/4 cup (60ml) mayonnaise
- 2 tablespoons (30ml) Worcestershire sauce
- 1 tablespoon (15ml) ketchup
- 1 teaspoon garlic powder
- 1/2 teaspoon paprika
- Fresh parsley, chopped (for garnish)

Instructions:

1. Preheat your oven to the temperature specified for your pizza dough (usually around 425°F or 220°C).
2. Roll out the pizza dough on a lightly floured surface to the desired size and thickness for your pizza.
3. Place string cheese sticks around the edge of the rolled-out dough, leaving a little space between each stick. Fold the dough over the cheese sticks and press to seal, creating a stuffed crust. Brush olive oil over the stuffed crust.

4. In a skillet, heat olive oil over medium-high heat. Add the thinly sliced onion and green bell pepper. Cook until softened and slightly caramelized, about 5-7 minutes. Remove from the skillet and set aside.
5. In the same skillet, add the thinly sliced beef steak. Season with salt and black pepper to taste. Cook until browned and cooked through, breaking it apart with a spatula as it cooks. Remove from heat and set aside.
6. In a small bowl, mix together the mayonnaise, Worcestershire sauce, ketchup, garlic powder, and paprika to make the sauce.
7. Spread the sauce evenly over the prepared pizza dough, leaving a small border around the edges for the crust.
8. Sprinkle shredded provolone cheese over the sauce.
9. Arrange the cooked onions, green bell peppers, and beef steak over the cheese.
10. Sprinkle shredded mozzarella cheese over the top.
11. Place the pizza in the preheated oven and bake according to the dough's instructions or until the crust is golden brown and the cheese is melted and bubbly.
12. Once the pizza is done baking, remove it from the oven and let it cool for a minute or two.
13. Garnish with chopped fresh parsley.
14. Slice the pizza and serve hot.

This Philly cheesesteak stuffed crust pizza is a delicious and satisfying meal that combines the flavors of a classic Philly cheesesteak with the cheesy goodness of pizza. Enjoy the combination of tender beef, sautéed onions and peppers, and melty cheese in every bite!

Roast Beef and Horseradish Pizza

Ingredients:

For the pizza dough:

- Pizza dough (store-bought or homemade)

For the toppings:

- 1 cup (240ml) sour cream
- 2-3 tablespoons prepared horseradish (adjust to taste)
- 1 tablespoon (15ml) olive oil
- 1 onion, thinly sliced
- 8 ounces (225g) thinly sliced roast beef
- 1 cup (150g) shredded mozzarella cheese
- 1/4 cup (30g) shredded Parmesan cheese
- Fresh parsley, chopped (for garnish)
- Salt and black pepper, to taste

Instructions:

1. Preheat your oven to the temperature specified for your pizza dough (usually around 425°F or 220°C).
2. Roll out the pizza dough on a lightly floured surface to your desired thickness.
3. In a small bowl, mix together the sour cream and prepared horseradish. Taste and adjust the amount of horseradish to your preference. Set aside.
4. In a skillet, heat olive oil over medium heat. Add the thinly sliced onion and cook until softened and caramelized, about 5-7 minutes. Remove from heat and set aside.
5. Spread a layer of the horseradish sour cream mixture over the rolled-out pizza dough, leaving a small border around the edges for the crust.
6. Arrange the thinly sliced roast beef over the horseradish sour cream mixture.
7. Spread the caramelized onions evenly over the roast beef.
8. Sprinkle shredded mozzarella cheese and shredded Parmesan cheese over the top.
9. Season with salt and black pepper to taste.

10. Place the pizza in the preheated oven and bake according to the dough's instructions or until the crust is golden brown and the cheese is melted and bubbly.
11. Once the pizza is done baking, remove it from the oven and let it cool for a minute or two.
12. Garnish with chopped fresh parsley.
13. Slice the pizza and serve hot.

This roast beef and horseradish pizza is a delicious and flavorful dish that combines the bold flavors of roast beef and horseradish with the creaminess of sour cream and the cheesy goodness of mozzarella and Parmesan. Enjoy the unique and delicious taste in every bite!

www.ingramcontent.com/pod-product-compliance
Lightning Source LLC
LaVergne TN
LVHW081608060526
838201LV00054B/2133